HBR'S 10 MUST READS

On
Diversity

HBR's 10 Must Reads series is the definitive collection of ideas and best practices for aspiring and experienced leaders alike. These books offer essential reading selected from the pages of *Harvard Business Review* on topics critical to the success of every manager.

Titles include:

HBR's 10 Must Reads 2015
HBR's 10 Must Reads 2016
HBR's 10 Must Reads 2017
HBR's 10 Must Reads 2018
HBR's 10 Must Reads 2019
HBR's 10 Must Reads 2020
HBR's 10 Must Reads for CEOs
HBR's 10 Must Reads for New Managers
HBR's 10 Must Reads on AI, Analytics, and the New Machine Age
HBR's 10 Must Reads on Business Model Innovation
HBR's 10 Must Reads on Change Management
HBR's 10 Must Reads on Collaboration
HBR's 10 Must Reads on Communication
HBR's 10 Must Reads on Diversity
HBR's 10 Must Reads on Emotional Intelligence
HBR's 10 Must Reads on Entrepreneurship and Startups
HBR's 10 Must Reads on Innovation
HBR's 10 Must Reads on Leadership
HBR's 10 Must Reads on Leadership for Healthcare
HBR's 10 Must Reads on Leadership Lessons from Sports
HBR's 10 Must Reads on Making Smart Decisions
HBR's 10 Must Reads on Managing Across Cultures
HBR's 10 Must Reads on Managing People
HBR's 10 Must Reads on Managing Yourself
HBR's 10 Must Reads on Mental Toughness
HBR's 10 Must Reads on Negotiation
HBR's 10 Must Reads on Nonprofits and the Social Sectors

On
Diversity

HARVARD BUSINESS REVIEW PRESS
Boston, Massachusetts

The web addresses referenced in this book were live and correct at the time of the book's publication but may be subject to change.

Library of Congress Cataloging-in-Publication Data

Title: HBR's 10 must reads on diversity.
Other titles: Harvard Business Review's ten must reads on diversity |
    Diversity | HBR's 10 must reads (Series)
Description: Boston, Massachusetts : Harvard Business Review Press, [2019]. |
    Series: HBR's 10 must reads series | Includes index.
Identifiers: LCCN 2018057865 | ISBN 9781633697720 (pbk.)
Subjects: LCSH: Diversity in the workplace. | Discrimination in employment.
Classification: LCC HF5549.5.M5 .H459 2019 | DDC 658.3008—dc23 LC record
available at https://lccn.loc.gov/2018057865

ISBN: 978-1-63369-772-0
eISBN: 978-1-63369-773-7

The paper used in this publication meets the requirements of the American National Standard for Permanence of Paper for Publications and Documents in Libraries and Archives Z39.48-1992.

Contents

On
Diversity

Making Differences Matter

A New Paradigm for Managing Diversity.
by David A. Thomas and Robin J. Ely

WHY SHOULD COMPANIES CONCERN THEMSELVES with diversity? Until recently, many managers answered this question with the assertion that discrimination is wrong, both legally and morally. But today managers are voicing a second notion as well. A more diverse workforce, they say, will increase organizational effectiveness. It will lift morale, bring greater access to new segments of the marketplace, and enhance productivity. In short, they claim, diversity will be good for business.

Yet if this is true—and we believe it is—where are the positive impacts of diversity? Numerous and varied initiatives to increase diversity in corporate America have been under way for more than two decades. Rarely, however, have those efforts spurred leaps in organizational effectiveness. Instead, many attempts to increase diversity in the workplace have backfired, sometimes even heightening tensions among employees and hindering a company's performance.

This article offers an explanation for why diversity efforts are not fulfilling their promise and presents a new paradigm for understanding—and leveraging—diversity. It is our belief that there is a distinct way to unleash the powerful benefits of a diverse workforce. Although these benefits include increased profitability, they go beyond financial measures to encompass learning, creativity, flexibility, organizational and individual growth, and the ability of a company to adjust rapidly and successfully to market changes. The desired transformation, however, requires a fundamental change in the attitudes and behaviors of an organization's leadership. And that will come only when senior managers abandon an underlying and flawed assumption about diversity and replace it with a broader understanding.

Most people assume that workplace diversity is about increasing racial, national, gender, or class representation—in other words, recruiting and retaining more people from traditionally underrepresented "identity groups." Taking this commonly held assumption as a starting point, we set out six years ago to investigate its link to organizational effectiveness. We soon found that thinking of diversity simply in terms of identity-group representation inhibited effectiveness.

Organizations usually take one of two paths in managing diversity. In the name of equality and fairness, they encourage (and expect) women and people of color to blend in. Or they set them apart in jobs that relate specifically to their backgrounds, assigning them, for example, to areas that require them to interface with clients or customers of the same identity group. African American MBA's often find themselves marketing products to inner-city communities; Hispanics frequently market to Hispanics or work for Latin American subsidiaries. In those kinds of cases, companies are operating on the assumption that the main virtue identity groups have to offer is a knowledge of their own people. This assumption is limited—and limiting—and detrimental to diversity efforts.

What we suggest here is that diversity goes beyond increasing the number of different identity-group affiliations on the payroll to recognizing that such an effort is merely the first step in managing a diverse workforce for the organization's utmost benefit. Diversity should be understood as *the varied perspectives and approaches to work* that members of different identity groups bring.

Idea in Brief

You know that workforce diversity is smart business: It opens markets, lifts morale, and enhances productivity. So why do most diversity initiatives backfire—heightening tensions and *hindering corporate performance?*

Many of us simply hire employees with diverse backgrounds—then await the payoff. We don't enable employees' differences to transform *how our organization does work.*

When employees use their differences to shape new goals, pro-cesses, leadership approaches, and teams, they bring more of themselves to work. They feel more committed to their jobs—and their companies grow.

How to activate this virtuous cycle? Transcend two existing diversity paradigms: **assimilation** ("we're all the same") or **differentiation** ("we celebrate differences"). Adopt a new paradigm—**integration**—that enables employees' differences to matter.

Women, Hispanics, Asian Americans, African Americans, Native Americans—these groups and others outside the mainstream of corporate America don't bring with them just their "insider information." They bring different, important, and competitively relevant knowledge and perspectives about how to actually *do work*—how to design processes, reach goals, frame tasks, create effective teams, communicate ideas, and lead. When allowed to, members of these groups can help companies grow and improve by challenging basic assumptions about an organization's functions, strategies, operations, practices, and procedures. And in doing so, they are able to bring more of their whole selves to the workplace and identify more fully with the work they do, setting in motion a virtuous circle. Certainly, individvuals can be expected to contribute to a company their firsthand familiarity with niche markets. But only when companies start thinking about diversity more holistically—as providing fresh and meaningful approaches to work—and stop assuming that diversity relates simply to how a person looks or where he or she comes from, will they be able to reap its full rewards.

Two perspectives have guided most diversity initiatives to date: the *discrimination-and-fairness paradigm* and the *access-and-legitimacy paradigm*. But we have identified a new, emerging

Idea in Practice

	Assimilation paradigm	Differentiation paradigm
Premise	"We're all the same."	"We celebrate differences."
Strategy	Hire diverse employees; encourage uniform behavior.	Match diverse employees to niche markets.
Advantage	Promotes fair hiring.	Expands markets.
Disadvantages	Subverting differences to encourage harmony, companies miss out on new ideas. Feeling detached from their work, employees' underperform.	Pigeonholed, staff can't influence mainstream work. Employees feel exploited and excluded from other opportunities.
Example	At a consulting company emphasizing quantitative analysis, minority managers encounter skepticism when they suggest interviewing clients. Labeling the incident as racial discord, the firm doesn't explore the potentially valuable new consulting approach.	To improve oversees operations, a U.S. bank assigns Europeans to its foreign offices. They excel—but the company doesn't know why. Not integrating diversity into its culture and practices, it becomes vulnerable: "If the French team resigns, what will we do?!"

approach to this complex management issue. This approach, which we call the *learning-and-effectiveness paradigm,* incorporates aspects of the first two paradigms but goes beyond them by concretely connecting diversity to approaches to work. Our goal is to help business leaders see what their own approach to diversity currently is and how it may already have influenced their companies' diversity efforts. Managers can learn to assess whether they need to

The Integration Paradigm

The **integration paradigm** *transcends* assimilation and differentiation—promoting equal opportunity *and* valuing cultural differences. Result? Employees' diverse perspectives positively impact companies' work.

> *Example*: A public-interest law firm's all-white staff's clients are exclusively white. It hires female attorneys of color, who encourage it to pursue litigation challenging English-only policies. Since such cases didn't fall under traditional affirmative-action work, the firm had ignored them. By taking them, it begins serving more women—immigrants—and enhances the quality of its work. The attorneys of color feel valued, and the firm attracts competent, diverse staff.

Additional suggestions for achieving integration:

1. **Encourage open discussion of cultural backgrounds.**

> *Example*: A food company's Chinese chemist draws on her cooking—not her scientific—experience to solve a soup-flavoring problem. But to fit in, she avoids sharing the real source of her inspiration with her colleagues—all white men. Open discussion of cultural differences would engage her more fully in work and workplace relationships.

2. **Eliminate all forms of dominance (by hierarchy, function, race, gender, etc.) that inhibit full contribution.** When one firm opened its annual strategy conference to people from all hierarchy levels, everyone knew their contributions were valued.

3. **Secure organizational trust.** In diverse workforces, people share more feelings and ideas. Tensions naturally arise. Demonstrate your commitment to diversity by acknowledging tensions—and resolving them swiftly.

change their diversity initiatives and, if so, how to accomplish that change.

The following discussion will also cite several examples of how connecting the new definition of diversity to the actual *doing* of work has led some organizations to markedly better performance. The organizations differ in many ways—none are in the same industry, for instance—but they are united by one similarity: Their leaders realize that increasing demographic variation does not in itself increase organizational effectiveness. They realize that it is *how* a company defines diversity—and *what it does* with the experiences of being a diverse organization—that delivers on the promise.

The Discrimination-and-Fairness Paradigm

Using the discrimination-and-fairness paradigm is perhaps thus far the dominant way of understanding diversity. Leaders who look at diversity through this lens usually focus on equal opportunity, fair treatment, recruitment, and compliance with federal Equal Employment Opportunity requirements. The paradigm's underlying logic can be expressed as follows:

> Prejudice has kept members of certain demographic groups out of organizations such as ours. As a matter of fairness and to comply with federal mandates, we need to work toward restructuring the makeup of our organization to let it more closely reflect that of society. We need managerial processes that ensure that all our employees are treated equally and with respect and that some are not given unfair advantage over others.

Although it resembles the thinking behind traditional affirmative-action efforts, the discrimination-and-fairness paradigm does go beyond a simple concern with numbers. Companies that operate with this philosophical orientation often institute mentoring and career-development programs specifically for the women and people of color in their ranks and train other employees to respect cultural differences. Under this paradigm, nevertheless, progress in diversity is measured by how well the company achieves its recruitment and retention goals rather than by the degree to which conditions in the company allow employees to draw on their personal assets and perspectives to do their work more effectively. The staff, one might say, gets diversified, but the work does not.

What are some of the common characteristics of companies that have used the discrimination-and-fairness paradigm successfully to increase their demographic diversity? Our research indicates that they are usually run by leaders who value due process and equal treatment of all employees and who have the authority to use top-down directives to enforce initiatives based on those attitudes. Such companies are often bureaucratic in structure, with control processes in place for monitoring, measuring, and rewarding individual performance. And finally, they are often organizations with entrenched, easily observable cultures, in which values like fairness are widespread and deeply inculcated and codes of conduct are clear and unambiguous. (Perhaps the most extreme example of an organization in which all these factors are at work is the United States Army.)

Without doubt, there are benefits to this paradigm: it does tend to increase demographic diversity in an organization, and it often succeeds in promoting fair treatment. But it also has significant limitations. The first of these is that its color-blind, gender-blind ideal is to some degree built on the implicit assumption that "we are all the same" or "we aspire to being all the same." Under this paradigm, it is not desirable for diversification of the workforce to influence the organization's work or culture. The company should operate as if every person were of the same race, gender, and nationality. It is unlikely that leaders who manage diversity under this paradigm will explore how people's differences generate a potential diversity of effective ways of working, leading, viewing the market, managing people, and learning.

Not only does the discrimination-and-fairness paradigm insist that everyone is the same, but, with its emphasis on equal treatment, it puts pressure on employees to make sure that important differences among them do not count. Genuine disagreements about work definition, therefore, are sometimes wrongly interpreted through this paradigm's fairness-unfairness lens—especially when honest disagreements are accompanied by tense debate. A female employee who insists, for example, that a company's advertising strategy is not appropriate for all ethnic segments in the marketplace might feel she is violating the code of assimilation upon which the paradigm is built. Moreover, if she were then to defend her opinion by citing, let us say, her personal knowledge of the ethnic group the company wanted to reach, she might risk being perceived as importing inappropriate attitudes into an organization that prides itself on being blind to cultural differences.

Workplace paradigms channel organizational thinking in powerful ways. By limiting the ability of employees to acknowledge openly their work-related but culturally based differences, the paradigm actually undermines the organization's capacity to learn about and improve its own strategies, processes, and practices. And it also keeps people from identifying strongly and personally with their work—a critical source of motivation and self-regulation in any business environment.

As an illustration of the paradigm's weaknesses, consider the case of Iversen Dunham, an international consulting firm that focuses on foreign and domestic economic-development policy. (Like all the examples in this article, the company is real, but its name is disguised.) Not long ago, the firm's managers asked us to help them understand why race relations had become a divisive issue precisely at a time when Iversen was receiving accolades for its diversity efforts. Indeed, other organizations had even begun to use the firm to benchmark their own diversity programs.

Iversen's diversity efforts had begun in the early 1970s, when senior managers decided to pursue greater racial and gender diversity in the firm's higher ranks. (The firm's leaders were strongly committed to the cause of social justice.) Women and people of color were hired and charted on career paths toward becoming project leaders. High performers among those who had left the firm were persuaded to return in senior roles. By 1989, about 50% of Iversen's project leaders and professionals were women, and 30% were people of color. The 13-member management committee, once exclusively white and male, included five women and four people of color. Additionally, Iversen had developed a strong contingent of foreign nationals.

It was at about this time, however, that tensions began to surface. Senior managers found it hard to believe that, after all the effort to create a fair and mutually respectful work community, some staff members could still be claiming that Iversen had racial discrimination problems. The management invited us to study the firm and deliver an outsider's assessment of its problem.

We had been inside the firm for only a short time when it became clear that Iversen's leaders viewed the dynamics of diversity through the lens of the discrimination-and-fairness paradigm. But where they saw racial discord, we discerned clashing approaches to the actual work of consulting. Why? Our research showed that tensions were strongest among midlevel project leaders. Surveys and interviews indicated that white project leaders welcomed demographic diversity as a general sign of progress but that they also thought the new employees were somehow changing the company, pulling it away from its original culture and its mission. Common criticisms were that African American and Hispanic staff made problems too complex by linking issues the organization had traditionally regarded as unrelated and that they brought on projects that seemed to require greater cultural sensitivity. White male project leaders also complained that their peers who were women and people of color were undermining one of Iversen's traditional strengths: its hard-core quantitative orientation. For instance, minority project leaders had suggested that Iversen consultants collect information and seek input from others in the client company besides senior managers—that is, from the rank and file and from middle managers. Some had urged Iversen to expand its consulting approach to include the gathering and analysis of qualitative data through interviewing and observation. Indeed, these project leaders had even challenged one of Iversen's long-standing, core assumptions: that the firm's reports were objective. They urged Iversen Dunham to recognize and address the subjective aspect of its analyses; the firm could, for example, include in its reports to clients dissenting Iversen views, if any existed.

For their part, project leaders who were women and people of color felt that they were not accorded the same level of authority to carry out that work as their white male peers. Moreover, they sensed that those peers were skeptical of their opinions, and they resented that doubts were not voiced openly.

Meanwhile, there also was some concern expressed about tension between white managers and nonwhite subordinates, who claimed they were being treated unfairly. But our analysis suggested that the manager-subordinate conflicts were not numerous enough

The Research

THIS ARTICLE IS BASED ON a three-part research effort that began in 1990. Our subject was diversity; but, more specifically, we sought to understand three management challenges under that heading. First, how do organizations successfully achieve and sustain racial and gender diversity in their executive and middle-management ranks? Second, what is the impact of diversity on an organization's practices, processes, and performance? And, finally, how do leaders influence whether diversity becomes an enhancing or detracting element in the organization?

Over the following six years, we worked particularly closely with three organizations that had attained a high degree of demographic diversity: a small urban law firm, a community bank, and a 200-person consulting firm. In addition, we studied nine other companies in varying stages of diversifying their workforces. The group included two financial-services firms, three *Fortune* 500 manufacturing companies, two midsize high-technology companies, a private foundation, and a university medical center. In each case, we based our analysis on interviews, surveys, archival data, and observation. It is from this work that the third paradigm for managing diversity emerged and with it our belief that old and limiting assumptions about the meaning of diversity must be abandoned before its true potential can be realized as a powerful way to increase organizational effectiveness.

---

to warrant the attention they were drawing from top management. We believed it was significant that senior managers found it easier to focus on this second type of conflict than on midlevel conflicts about project choice and project definition. Indeed, Iversen Dunham's focus seemed to be a result of the firm's reliance on its particular diversity paradigm and the emphasis on fairness and equality. It was relatively easy to diagnose problems in light of those concepts and to devise a solution: just get managers to treat their subordinates more fairly.

In contrast, it was difficult to diagnose peer-to-peer tensions in the framework of this model. Such conflicts were about the very nature of Iversen's work, not simply unfair treatment. Yes, they were related to identity-group affiliations, but they were not symptomatic of classic racism. It was Iversen's paradigm that led managers to interpret them as such. Remember, we were asked to assess what was supposed to be a racial discrimination problem. Iversen's discrimination-and-fairness paradigm had created a kind of cognitive blind spot; and, as a result, the company's leadership could not frame the problem accurately or solve it effectively. Instead, the company needed a cultural shift—it needed to grasp what to do with its diversity once it had achieved the numbers. If all Iversen Dunham employees were to contribute to the fullest extent, the company would need a paradigm that would encourage open and explicit discussion of what identity-group differences really mean and how they can be used as sources of individual and organizational effectiveness.

Today, mainly because of senior managers' resistance to such a cultural transformation, Iversen continues to struggle with the tensions arising from the diversity of its workforce.

The Access-and-Legitimacy Paradigm

In the competitive climate of the 1980s and 1990s, a new rhetoric and rationale for managing diversity emerged. If the discrimination-and-fairness paradigm can be said to have idealized assimilation and color- and gender-blind conformism, the access-and-legitimacy paradigm was predicated on the acceptance and celebration of differences. The underlying motivation of the access-and-legitimacy paradigm can be expressed this way:

> We are living in an increasingly multicultural country, and new ethnic groups are quickly gaining consumer power. Our company needs a demographically more diverse workforce to help us gain access to these differentiated segments. We need employees with multilingual skills in order to understand and serve our customers better and to gain legitimacy with them. Diversity isn't just fair; it makes business sense.

Where this paradigm has taken hold, organizations have pushed for access to—and legitimacy with—a more diverse clientele by matching the demographics of the organization to those of critical consumer or constituent groups. In some cases, the effort has led to substantial increases in organizational diversity. In investment banks, for example, municipal finance departments have long led corporate finance departments in pursuing demographic diversity because of the typical makeup of the administration of city halls and county boards. Many consumer-products companies that have used market segmentation based on gender, racial, and other demographic differences have also frequently created dedicated marketing positions for each segment. The paradigm has therefore led to new professional and managerial opportunities for women and people of color.

What are the common characteristics of organizations that have successfully used the access-and-legitimacy paradigm to increase their demographic diversity? There is but one: such companies almost always operate in a business environment in which there is increased diversity among customers, clients, or the labor pool—and therefore a clear opportunity or an imminent threat to the company.

Again, the paradigm has its strengths. Its market-based motivation and the potential for competitive advantage that it suggests are often qualities an entire company can understand and therefore support. But the paradigm is perhaps more notable for its limitations. In their pursuit of niche markets, access-and-legitimacy organizations tend to emphasize the role of cultural differences in a company without really analyzing those differences to see how they actually affect the work that is done. Whereas discrimination-and-fairness leaders are too quick to subvert differences in the interest of preserving harmony, access-and-legitimacy leaders are too quick to push staff with niche capabilities into differentiated pigeonholes without trying to understand what those capabilities really are and how they could be integrated into the company's mainstream work. To illustrate our point, we present the case of Access Capital.

Access Capital International is a U.S. investment bank that in the early 1980s launched an aggressive plan to expand into Europe. Initially, however, Access encountered serious problems opening offices in international markets; the people from the United States who were installed abroad lacked credibility, were ignorant of local cultural norms and market conditions, and simply couldn't seem to connect with native clients. Access responded by hiring Europeans who had attended North American business schools and by assigning them in teams to the foreign offices. This strategy was a marked success. Before long, the leaders of Access could take enormous pride in the fact that their European operations were highly profitable and staffed by a truly international corps of professionals. They took to calling the company "the best investment bank in the world."

Several years passed. Access's foreign offices continued to thrive, but some leaders were beginning to sense that the company was not fully benefiting from its diversity efforts. Indeed, some even suspected that the bank had made itself vulnerable because of how it had chosen to manage diversity. A senior executive from the United States explains:

If the French team all resigned tomorrow, what would we do? I'm not sure what we *could* do! We've never attempted to learn what these differences and cultural competencies really are, how they change the process of doing business. What is the German country team actually doing? We don't know. We know they're good, but we don't know the subtleties of how they do what they do. We assumed—and I think correctly—that culture makes a difference, but that's about as far as we went. We hired Europeans with American MBA's because we didn't know why we couldn't do business in Europe—we just assumed there was something cultural about why we couldn't connect. And ten years later, we still don't know what it is. If we knew, then perhaps we could take it and teach it. Which part of the investment banking process is universal and which part of it draws upon particular cultural competencies? What are the commonalities and differences? I may not be German, but maybe I could do better at understanding what it means to be an American doing business in Germany. Our company's biggest failing is that the department heads in London and the directors of the various country teams have never talked about these cultural identity issues openly. We knew enough to *use* people's cultural strengths, as it were, but we never seemed to learn from them.

Access's story makes an important point about the main limitation of the access-and-legitimacy paradigm: under its influence, the motivation for diversity usually emerges from very immediate and often crisis-oriented needs for access and legitimacy—in this case, the need to broker deals in European markets. However, once the organization appears to be achieving its goal, the leaders seldom go on to identify and analyze the culturally based skills, beliefs, and practices that worked so well. Nor do they consider how the organization can incorporate and learn from those skills, beliefs, or practices in order to capitalize on diversity in the long run.

Under the access-and-legitimacy paradigm, it was as if the bank's country teams had become little spin-off companies in their own right, doing their own exotic, slightly mysterious cultural-diversity thing in a niche market of their own, using competencies that for some reason could not become more fully integrated into the larger organization's understanding of itself. Difference was valued within Access Capital—hence the development of country teams in the first place—but not valued enough that the organization would try to integrate it into the very core of its culture and into its business practices.

Finally, the access-and-legitimacy paradigm can leave some employees feeling exploited. Many organizations using this paradigm have diversified only in those areas in which they interact with particular niche-market segments. In time, many individuals recruited for this function have come to feel devalued and used as they begin to sense that opportunities in other parts of the organization are closed to them. Often the larger organization regards the experience of these employees as more limited or specialized, even though many of them in fact started their careers in the mainstream market before moving to special markets where their cultural backgrounds were a recognized asset. Also, many of these people say that when companies have needed to downsize or narrow their marketing focus, it is the special departments that are often the first to go. That situation creates tenuous and ultimately untenable career paths for employees in the special departments.

The Emerging Paradigm: Connecting Diversity to Work Perspectives

Recently, in the course of our research, we have encountered a small number of organizations that, having relied initially on one of the above paradigms to guide their diversity efforts, have come to believe that they are not making the most of their own pluralism. These organizations, like Access Capital, recognize that employees frequently make decisions and choices at work that draw upon their cultural background—choices made because of their identity-group affiliations. The companies have also developed an outlook on diversity that enables them to *incorporate* employees' perspectives into the main work of the organization and to enhance work by re-thinking primary tasks and redefining markets, products, strategies, missions, business practices, and even cultures. Such companies are using the learning-and-effectiveness paradigm for managing diversity and, by doing so, are tapping diversity's true benefits.

A case in point is Dewey & Levin, a small public-interest law firm located in a northeastern U.S. city. Although Dewey & Levin had long been a profitable practice, by the mid-1980s its all-white legal staff had become concerned that the women they represented in employment-related disputes were exclusively white. The firm's attorneys viewed that fact as a deficiency in light of their mandate to advocate on behalf of all women. Using the thinking behind the access-and-legitimacy paradigm, they also saw it as bad for business.

Shortly thereafter, the firm hired a Hispanic female attorney. The partners' hope, simply put, was that she would bring in clients from her own community and also demonstrate the firm's commitment to representing all women. But something even bigger than that happened. The new attorney introduced ideas to Dewey & Levin about what kinds of cases it should take on. Senior managers were open to those ideas and pursued them with great success. More women of color were hired, and they, too, brought fresh perspectives. The firm now pursues cases that its previously all-white legal staff would not have thought relevant or appropriate because the link between the firm's mission and the employment issues involved in the cases would not have been obvious to them. For example, the firm has pursued precedent-setting litigation that challenges English-only policies—an area that it once would have ignored because such policies did not fall under the purview of traditional affirmative-action work. Yet it now sees a link between English-only policies and employment issues for a large group of women—primarily recent immigrants—whom it had previously failed to serve adequately. As one of the white principals explains, the demographic composition of Dewey & Levin "has affected the work in terms of expanding notions of what are [relevant] issues and taking on issues and framing them in creative ways that would have never been done [with an all-white staff]. It's really changed the substance—and in that sense enhanced the quality—of our work."

Dewey & Levin's increased business success has reinforced its commitment to diversity. In addition, people of color at the firm uniformly report feeling respected, not simply "brought along as window dressing." Many of the new attorneys say their perspectives are heard with a kind of openness and interest they have never experienced before in a work setting. Not surprisingly, the firm has had little difficulty attracting and retaining a competent and diverse professional staff.

If the discrimination-and-fairness paradigm is organized around the theme of assimilation—in which the aim is to achieve a demographically representative workforce whose members treat one another exactly the same—then the access-and-legitimacy paradigm can be regarded as coalescing around an almost opposite concept: differentiation, in which the objective is to place different people where their demographic characteristics match those of important constituents and markets.

The emerging paradigm, in contrast to both, organizes itself around the overarching theme of integration. Assimilation goes too far in pursuing sameness. Differentiation, as we have shown, overshoots in the other direction. The new model for managing diversity transcends both. Like the fairness paradigm, it promotes equal opportunity for all individuals. And like the access paradigm, it acknowledges cultural differences among people and recognizes the value in those differences. Yet this new model for managing diversity lets the organization internalize differences among employees so that it learns and grows because of them. Indeed, with the model fully in place, members of the organization can say, We are all on the same team, *with* our differences—not *despite* them.

Eight Preconditions for Making the Paradigm Shift

Dewey & Levin may be atypical in its eagerness to open itself up to change and engage in a long-term transformation process. We remain convinced, however, that unless organizations that are currently in the grip of the other two paradigms can revise their view of diversity so as to avoid cognitive blind spots, opportunities will be missed, tensions will most likely be misdiagnosed, and companies will continue to find the potential benefits of diversity elusive.

Hence the question arises: What is it about the law firm of Dewey & Levin and other emerging third-paradigm companies that enables them to make the most of their diversity? Our research suggests that there are eight preconditions that help to position organizations to use identity-group differences in the service of organizational learning, growth, and renewal.

1. **The leadership must understand that a diverse workforce will embody different perspectives and approaches to work, and must truly value variety of opinion and insight.** We know of a financial services company that once assumed that the only successful sales model was one that utilized aggressive, rapid-fire cold calls. (Indeed, its incentive system rewarded salespeople in large part for the number of calls made.) An internal review of the company's diversity initiatives, however, showed that the company's first- and third-most-profitable employees were women who were most likely to use a sales technique based on the slow but sure building of relationships. The company's top management has now made the link between different identity groups and different approaches to how work gets done and has come to see that there is more than one right way to get positive results.

2. **The leadership must recognize both the learning opportunities and the challenges that the expression of different perspectives presents for an organization.** In other words, the second precondition is a leadership that is committed to persevering during the long process of learning and relearning that the new paradigm requires.

3. **The organizational culture must create an expectation of high standards of performance from everyone.** Such a culture isn't one that expects less from some employees than from others. Some organizations expect women and people of color to underperform—a negative assumption that too often becomes a self-fulfilling prophecy. To move to the third paradigm, a company must believe that all its members can and should contribute fully.

4. **The organizational culture must stimulate personal development.** Such a culture brings out people's full range of useful knowledge and skills—usually through the careful design of jobs that allow people to grow and develop but also through training and education programs.

5. **The organizational culture must encourage openness.** Such a culture instills a high tolerance for debate and supports constructive conflict on work-related matters.

6. **The culture must make workers feel valued.** If this precondition is met, workers feel committed to—and empowered within—the organization and therefore feel comfortable taking the initiative to apply their skills and experiences in new ways to enhance their job performance.

7. **The organization must have a well-articulated and widely understood mission.** Such a mission enables people to be clear about what the company is trying to accomplish. It grounds and guides discussions about work-related changes that staff members might

suggest. Being clear about the company's mission helps keep discussions about work differences from degenerating into debates about the validity of people's perspectives. A clear mission provides a focal point that keeps the discussion centered on accomplishment of goals.

8. The organization must have a relatively egalitarian, nonbureaucratic structure. It's important to have a structure that promotes the exchange of ideas and welcomes constructive challenges to the usual way of doing things—from any employee with valuable experience. Forward-thinking leaders in bureaucratic organizations must retain the organization's efficiency-promoting control systems and chains of command while finding ways to reshape the change-resisting mind-set of the classic bureaucratic model. They need to separate the enabling elements of bureaucracy (the ability to get things done) from the disabling elements of bureaucracy (those that create resistance to experimentation).

First Interstate Bank: A Paradigm Shift in Progress

All eight preconditions do not have to be in place in order to begin a shift from the first or second diversity orientations toward the learning-and-effectiveness paradigm. But most should be. First Interstate Bank, a midsize bank operating in a midwestern city, illustrates this point.

First Interstate, admittedly, is not a typical bank. Its client base is a minority community, and its mission is expressly to serve that base through "the development of a highly talented workforce." The bank is unique in other ways: its leadership welcomes constructive criticism; its structure is relatively egalitarian and nonbureaucratic; and its culture is open-minded. Nevertheless, First Interstate had long enforced a policy that loan officers had to hold college degrees. Those without were hired only for support-staff jobs and were never promoted beyond or outside support functions.

Two years ago, however, the support staff began to challenge the policy. Many of them had been with First Interstate for many years and, with the company's active support, had improved their skills through training. Others had expanded their skills on the job, again with the bank's encouragement, learning to run credit checks, prepare presentations for clients, and even calculate the algorithms necessary for many loan decisions. As a result, some people on the support staff were doing many of the same tasks as loan officers. Why, then, they wondered, couldn't they receive commensurate rewards in title and compensation?

This questioning led to a series of contentious meetings between the support staff and the bank's senior managers. It soon became clear that the problem called for managing diversity—diversity based not on race or gender but on class. The support personnel were uniformly from lower socioeconomic communities than were the college-educated loan officers. Regardless, the principle was the same as for race-or gender-based diversity problems. The support staff had different ideas about how the work of the bank should be done. They argued that those among them with the requisite skills should be allowed to rise through the ranks to professional positions, and they believed their ideas were not being heard or accepted.

Their beliefs challenged assumptions that the company's leadership had long held about which employees should have the authority to deal with customers and about how much responsibility administrative employees should ultimately receive. In order to take up this challenge, the bank would have to be open to exploring the requirements that a new perspective would impose on it. It would need to consider the possibility of mapping out an educational and career path for people without degrees—a path that could put such workers on the road to becoming loan officers. In other words, the leadership would have to transform itself willingly and embrace fluidity in policies that in times past had been clearly stated and unquestioningly held.

Today the bank's leadership is undergoing just such a transformation. The going, however, is far from easy. The bank's senior managers now must look beyond the tensions and acrimony sparked by the debate over differing work perspectives and consider the bank's new direction an important learning and growth opportunity.

Shift Complete: Third-Paradigm Companies in Action

First Interstate is a shift in progress; but, in addition to Dewey & Levin, there are several organizations we know of for which the shift is complete. In these cases, company leaders have played a critical role as facilitators and tone setters. We have observed in particular that in organizations that have adopted the new perspective, leaders and managers—and, following in their tracks, employees in general—are taking four kinds of action.

They are making the mental connection

First, in organizations that have adopted the new perspective, the leaders are actively seeking opportunities to explore how identity-group differences affect relationships among workers and affect the way work gets done. They are investing considerable time and energy in understanding how identity-group memberships take on social meanings in the organization and how those meanings manifest themselves in the way work is defined, assigned, and accomplished. When there is no proactive search to understand, then learning from diversity, if it happens at all, can occur only reactively—that is, in response to diversity-related crises.

The situation at Iversen Dunham illustrates the missed opportunities resulting from that scenario. Rather than seeing differences in the way project leaders defined and approached their work as an opportunity to gain new insights and develop new approaches to achieving its mission, the firm remained entrenched in its traditional ways, able to arbitrate such differences only by thinking about what was fair and what was racist. With this quite limited view of the role race can play in an organization, discussions about the topic become fraught with fear and defensiveness, and everyone misses out on insights about how race might influence work in positive ways.

A second case, however, illustrates how some leaders using the new paradigm have been able to envision—and make—the connection between cultural diversity and the company's work. A vice president of Mastiff, a large national insurance company, received a complaint from one of the managers in her unit, an African American man. The manager wanted to demote an African American woman he had hired for a leadership position from another Mastiff division just three months before. He told the vice president he was profoundly disappointed with the performance of his new hire.

"I hired her because I was pretty certain she had tremendous leadership skill," he said. "I knew she had a management style that was very open and empowering. I was also sure she'd have a great impact on the rest of the management team. But she hasn't done any of that."

Surprised, the vice president tried to find out from him what he thought the problem was, but she was not getting any answers that she felt really defined or illuminated the root of the problem. Privately, it puzzled her that someone would decide to demote a 15-year veteran of the company—and a minority woman at that—so soon after bringing her to his unit.

The vice president probed further. In the course of the conversation, the manager happened to mention that he knew the new employee from church and was familiar with the way she handled leadership there and in other community settings. In those less formal situations, he had seen her perform as an extremely effective, sensitive, and influential leader.

That is when the vice president made an interpretive leap. "If that's what you know about her," the vice president said to the manager, "then the question for us is, why can't she bring those skills to work here?" The vice president decided to arrange a meeting with all three present to ask this very question directly. In the meeting, the African American woman explained, "I didn't think I would last long if I acted that way here. My personal style of leadership—that particular style—works well if you have the permission to do it fully; then you can just do it and not have to look over your shoulder."

Pointing to the manager who had planned to fire her, she added, "He's right. The style of leadership I use outside this company can definitely be effective. But I've been at Mastiff for 15 years. I know this organization, and I know if I brought that piece of myself—if I became that authentic—I just wouldn't survive here."

What this example illustrates is that the vice president's learning-and-effectiveness paradigm led her to explore and then make the link between cultural diversity and work style. What was occurring, she realized, was a mismatch between the cultural background of the recently promoted woman and the cultural environment of her work setting. It had little to do with private attitudes or feelings, or gender issues, or some inherent lack of leadership ability. The source of the underperformance was that the newly promoted woman had a certain style and the organization's culture did not support her in expressing it comfortably. The vice president's paradigm led her to ask new questions and to seek out new information, but, more important, it also led her to interpret existing information differently.

The two senior managers began to realize that part of the African American woman's inability to see herself as a leader at work was that she had for so long been undervalued in the organization. And, in a sense, she had become used to splitting herself off from who she was in her own community. In the 15 years she had been at Mastiff, she had done her job well as an individual contributor, but she had never received any signals that her bosses wanted her to draw on her cultural competencies in order to lead effectively.

They are legitimating open discussion
Leaders and managers who have adopted the new paradigm are taking the initiative to "green light" open discussion about how identity-group memberships inform and influence an employee's experience and the organization's behavior. They are encouraging people to make *explicit* use of background cultural experience and the pools of knowledge gained outside the organization to inform and enhance their work. Individuals often do use their cultural competencies at work, but in a closeted, almost embarrassed, way. The unfortunate result is that the opportunity for collective and organizational learning and improvement is lost.

The case of a Chinese woman who worked as a chemist at Torinno Food Company illustrates this point. Linda was part of a product development group at Torinno when a problem arose with the flavoring of a new soup. After the group had made a number of scientific attempts to correct the problem, Linda came up with the solution by "setting aside my chemistry and drawing on my understanding of Chinese cooking." She did not, however, share with her colleagues—all of them white males—the real source of her inspiration for the solution for fear that it would set her apart or that they might consider her unprofessional. Overlaid on the cultural issue, of course, was a gender issue (women cooking) as well as a work-family issue (women doing *home* cooking in a chemistry lab). All of these themes had erected unspoken boundaries that Linda knew could be career-damaging for her to cross. After solving the problem, she simply went back to the so-called scientific way of doing things.

Senior managers at Torinno Foods in fact had made a substantial commitment to diversifying the workforce through a program designed to teach employees to value the contributions of all its members. Yet Linda's perceptions indicate that, in the actual day-to-day context of work, the program had failed—and in precisely one of those areas where it would have been important for it to have worked. It had failed to affirm someone's identity-group experiences as a legitimate source of insight into her work. It is likely that this organization will miss future opportunities to take full advantage of the talent of employees such as Linda. When people believe that they must suggest and apply their ideas covertly, the organization also misses opportunities to discuss, debate, refine, and build on those ideas fully. In addition, because individuals like Linda will continue to think that they must hide parts of themselves in order to fit in, they will find it difficult to engage fully not only in their work but also in their workplace relationships. That kind of situation can breed resentment and misunderstanding, fueling tensions that can further obstruct productive work relationships.

They actively work against forms of dominance and subordination that inhibit full contribution

Companies in which the third paradigm is emerging have leaders and managers who take responsibility for removing the barriers that block employees from using the full range of their competencies, cultural or otherwise. Racism, homophobia, sexism, and sexual harassment are the most obvious forms of dominance that decrease individual and organizational effectiveness—and third-paradigm leaders have zero tolerance for them. In addition, the leaders are aware that organizations can create their own unique patterns of dominance and subordination based on the presumed superiority and entitlement of some groups over others. It is not uncommon, for instance, to find organizations in which one functional area considers itself better than another. Members of the presumed inferior group frequently describe the organization in the very terms used by those who experience identity-group discrimination. Regardless of the source of the oppression, the result is diminished performance and commitment from employees.

What can leaders do to prevent those kinds of behaviors beyond explicitly forbidding any forms of dominance? They can and should test their own assumptions about the competencies of all members of the workforce because negative assumptions are often unconsciously communicated in powerful—albeit nonverbal—ways. For example, senior managers at Delta Manufacturing had for years allowed productivity and quality at their inner-city plants to lag well behind the levels of other plants. When the company's chief executive officer began to question why the problem was never addressed, he came to realize that, in his heart, he had believed that inner-city workers, most of whom were African American or Hispanic, were not capable of doing better than subpar. In the end, the CEO and his senior management team were able to reverse their reasoning and take responsibility for improving the situation. The result was a sharp increase in the performance of the inner-city plants and a message to the entire organization about the capabilities of its entire workforce.

At Mastiff, the insurance company discussed earlier, the vice president and her manager decided to work with the recently promoted African American woman rather than demote her. They realized that their unit was really a pocket inside the larger organization: they did not have to wait for the rest of the organization to make a paradigm shift in order for their particular unit to change. So they met again to think about how to create conditions within their unit that would move the woman toward seeing her leadership position as encompassing all her skills. They assured her that her authentic style of leadership was precisely what they wanted her to bring to the job. They wanted her to be able to use whatever aspects of herself she thought would make her more effective in her work because the whole purpose was to do the job effectively, not to fit some preset traditional formula of how to behave. They let her know that, as a management team, they would try to adjust and change and support her. And they would deal with whatever consequences resulted from her exercising her decision rights in new ways.

Another example of this line of action—working against forms of dominance and subordination to enable full contribution—is the way the CEO of a major chemical company modified the attendance rules for his company's annual strategy conference. In the past, the conference had been attended only by senior executives, a relatively homogeneous group of white men. The company had been working hard on increasing the representation of women and people of color in its ranks, and the CEO could have left it at that. But he reckoned that, unless steps were taken, it would be ten years before the conferences tapped into the insights and perspectives of his newly diverse workforce. So he took the bold step of opening the conference to people from across all levels of the hierarchy, bringing together a diagonal slice of the organization. He also asked the conference organizers to come up with specific interventions, such as small group meetings before the larger session, to ensure that the new attendees would be comfortable enough to enter discussions. The result was that strategy-conference participants heard a much broader, richer, and livelier discussion about future scenarios for the company.

They are making sure that organizational trust stays intact
Few things are faster at killing a shift to a new way of thinking about diversity than feelings of broken trust. Therefore, managers of organizations that are successfully shifting to the learning-and-effectiveness paradigm take one more step: they make sure their organizations remain "safe" places for employees to be themselves. These manag-

ers recognize that tensions naturally arise as an organization begins to make room for diversity, starts to experiment with process and product ideas, and learns to reappraise its mission in light of suggestions from newly empowered constituents in the company. But as people put more of themselves out and open up about new feelings and ideas, the dynamics of the learning-and-effectiveness paradigm can produce temporary vulnerabilities. Managers who have helped their organizations make the change successfully have consistently demonstrated their commitment to the process and to all employees by setting a tone of honest discourse, by acknowledging tensions, and by resolving them sensitively and swiftly.

Our research over the past six years indicates that one cardinal limitation is at the root of companies' inability to attain the expected performance benefits of higher levels of diversity: the leadership's vision of the purpose of a diversified workforce. We have described the two most dominant orientations toward diversity and some of their consequences and limitations, together with a new framework for understanding and managing diversity. The learning-and-effectiveness paradigm we have outlined here is, undoubtedly, still in an emergent phase in those few organizations that embody it. We expect that as more organizations take on the challenge of truly engaging their diversity, new and unforeseen dilemmas will arise. Thus, perhaps more than anything else, a shift toward this paradigm requires a high-level commitment to learning more about the environment, structure, and tasks of one's organization, and giving improvement-generating change greater priority than the security of what is familiar. This is not an easy challenge, but we remain convinced that unless organizations take this step, any diversity initiative will fall short of fulfilling its rich promise.

Originally published in September–October 1996. Reprint 96510

Why Diversity Programs Fail

by Frank Dobbin and Alexandra Kalev

BUSINESSES STARTED CARING A LOT more about diversity after a series of high-profile lawsuits rocked the financial industry. In the late 1990s and early 2000s, Morgan Stanley shelled out $54 million—and Smith Barney and Merrill Lynch more than $100 million each—to settle sex discrimination claims. In 2007, Morgan was back at the table, facing a new class action, which cost the company $46 million. In 2013, Bank of America Merrill Lynch settled a race discrimination suit for $160 million. Cases like these brought Merrill's total 15-year payout to nearly *half a billion* dollars.

It's no wonder that Wall Street firms now require new hires to sign arbitration contracts agreeing not to join class actions. They have also expanded training and other diversity programs. But on balance, equality isn't improving in financial services or elsewhere. Although the proportion of managers at U.S. commercial banks who were Hispanic rose from 4.7% in 2003 to 5.7% in 2014, white women's representation dropped from 39% to 35%, and black men's from 2.5% to 2.3%. The numbers were even worse in investment banks (though that industry is shrinking, which complicates the analysis). Among all U.S. companies with 100 or more employees, the proportion of black men in management increased just slightly—from 3% to 3.3%—from 1985 to 2014. White women saw bigger gains from 1985 to 2000—rising from 22% to 29% of managers—but their numbers haven't budged since then. Even in Silicon Valley, where many leaders tout the need to increase diversity for both business and social justice reasons, bread-and-butter tech jobs remain dominated by white men.

It shouldn't be surprising that most diversity programs aren't increasing diversity. Despite a few new bells and whistles, courtesy of big data, companies are basically doubling down on the same approaches they've used since the 1960s—which often make things worse, not better. Firms have long relied on diversity training to reduce bias on the job, hiring tests and performance ratings to limit it in recruitment and promotions, and grievance systems to give employees a way to challenge managers. Those tools are designed to preempt lawsuits by policing managers' thoughts and actions. Yet laboratory studies show that this kind of force-feeding can activate bias rather than stamp it out. As social scientists have found, people often rebel against rules to assert their autonomy. Try to coerce me to do X, Y, or Z, and I'll do the opposite just to prove that I'm my own person.

In analyzing three decades' worth of data from more than 800 U.S. firms and interviewing hundreds of line managers and executives at length, we've seen that companies get better results when they ease up on the control tactics. It's more effective to engage managers in solving the problem, increase their on-the-job contact with female and minority workers, and promote social accountability—the desire to look fair-minded. That's why interventions such as targeted college recruitment, mentoring programs, self-managed teams, and task forces have boosted diversity in businesses. Some of the most effective solutions aren't even designed with diversity in mind.

Here, we dig into the data, the interviews, and company examples to shed light on what doesn't work and what does.

Why You Can't Just Outlaw Bias

Executives favor a classic command-and-control approach to diversity because it boils expected behaviors down to dos and don'ts that are easy to understand and defend. Yet this approach also flies in the face of nearly everything we know about how to motivate people to

Idea in Brief

The Problem

To reduce bias and increase diversity, organizations are relying on the same programs they've been using since the 1960s. Some of these efforts make matters worse, not better.

The Reason

Most diversity programs focus on controlling managers' behavior, and as studies show, that approach tends to activate bias rather than quash it. People rebel against rules that threaten their autonomy.

The Solution

Instead of trying to police managers' decisions, the most effective programs engage people in working for diversity, increase their contact with women and minorities, and tap into their desire to look good to others.

make changes. Decades of social science research point to a simple truth: You won't get managers on board by blaming and shaming them with rules and reeducation. Let's look at how the most common top-down efforts typically go wrong.

Diversity training

Do people who undergo training usually shed their biases? Researchers have been examining that question since before World War II, in nearly a thousand studies. It turns out that while people are easily taught to respond correctly to a questionnaire about bias, they soon forget the right answers. The positive effects of diversity training rarely last beyond a day or two, and a number of studies suggest that it can activate bias or spark a backlash. Nonetheless, nearly half of midsize companies use it, as do nearly all the *Fortune* 500.

Many firms see adverse effects. One reason is that three-quarters use negative messages in their training. By headlining the legal case for diversity and trotting out stories of huge settlements, they issue an implied threat: "Discriminate, and the company will pay the price." We understand the temptation—that's how we got your attention in the first paragraph—but threats, or "negative incentives," don't win converts.

Another reason is that about three-quarters of firms with training still follow the dated advice of the late diversity guru R. Roosevelt

Thomas Jr. "If diversity management is strategic to the organization," he used to say, diversity training must be mandatory, and management has to make it clear that "if you can't deal with that, then we have to ask you to leave." But five years after instituting required training for managers, companies saw no improvement in the proportion of white women, black men, and Hispanics in management, and the share of black women actually decreased by 9%, on average, while the ranks of Asian-American men and women shrank by 4% to 5%. Trainers tell us that people often respond to compulsory courses with anger and resistance—and many participants actually report more animosity toward other groups afterward.

But voluntary training evokes the opposite response ("I chose to show up, so I must be pro-diversity"), leading to better results: increases of 9% to 13% in black men, Hispanic men, and Asian-American men and women in management five years out (with no decline in white or black women). Research from the University of Toronto reinforces our findings: In one study white subjects read a brochure critiquing prejudice toward blacks. When people felt pressure to agree with it, the reading strengthened their bias against blacks. When they felt the choice was theirs, the reading reduced bias.

Companies too often signal that training is remedial. The diversity manager at a national beverage company told us that the top brass uses it to deal with problem groups. "If there are a number of complaints . . . or, God forbid, some type of harassment case . . . leaders say, 'Everyone in the business unit will go through it again.'" Most companies with training have special programs for managers. To be sure, they're a high-risk group because they make the hiring, promotion, and pay decisions. But singling them out implies that they're the worst culprits. Managers tend to resent that implication and resist the message.

Hiring tests

Some 40% of companies now try to fight bias with mandatory hiring tests assessing the skills of candidates for frontline jobs. But managers don't like being told that they can't hire whomever they please, and our research suggests that they often use the tests selectively. Back in the 1950s, following the postwar migration of blacks northward, Swift & Company, Chicago meatpackers, instituted tests for supervisor and quality-checking jobs. One study found managers telling blacks that they had failed the test and then promoting whites who hadn't been tested. A black machine operator reported: "I had four years at Englewood High School. I took an exam for a checker's job. The foreman told me I failed" and gave the job to a white man who "didn't take the exam."

This kind of thing still happens. When we interviewed the new HR director at a West Coast food company, he said he found that white managers were making only strangers—most of them minorities—take supervisor tests and hiring white friends without testing them. "If you are going to test one person for this particular job title," he told us, "you need to test everybody."

But even managers who test everyone applying for a position may ignore the results. Investment banks and consulting firms build tests into their job interviews, asking people to solve math and scenario-based problems on the spot. While studying this practice, Kellogg professor Lauren Rivera played a fly on the wall during hiring meetings at one firm. She found that the team paid little attention when white men blew the math test but close attention when women and blacks did. Because decision makers (deliberately or not) cherry-picked results, the testing amplified bias rather than quashed it.

Companies that institute written job tests for managers—about 10% have them today—see decreases of 4% to 10% in the share of managerial jobs held by white women, African-American men and women, Hispanic men and women, and Asian-American women over the next five years. There are significant declines among white and Asian-American women—groups with high levels of education, which typically score well on standard managerial tests. So group differences in test-taking skills don't explain the pattern.

Performance ratings
More than 90% of midsize and large companies use annual performance ratings to ensure that managers make fair pay and promotion

decisions. Identifying and rewarding the best workers isn't the only goal—the ratings also provide a litigation shield. Companies sued for discrimination often claim that their performance rating systems prevent biased treatment.

But studies show that raters tend to lowball women and minorities in performance reviews. And some managers give everyone high marks to avoid hassles with employees or to keep their options open when handing out promotions. However managers work around performance systems, the bottom line is that ratings don't boost diversity. When companies introduce them, there's no effect on minority managers over the next five years, and the share of white women in management drops by 4%, on average.

Grievance procedures

This last tactic is meant to identify and rehabilitate biased managers. About half of midsize and large firms have systems through which employees can challenge pay, promotion, and termination decisions. But many managers—rather than change their own behavior or address discrimination by others—try to get even with or belittle employees who complain. Among the nearly 90,000 discrimination complaints made to the Equal Employment Opportunity Commission in 2015, 45% included a charge of retaliation—which suggests that the original report was met with ridicule, demotion, or worse.

Once people see that a grievance system isn't warding off bad behavior in their organization, they may become less likely to speak up. Indeed, employee surveys show that most people don't report discrimination. This leads to another unintended consequence: Managers who receive few complaints conclude that their firms don't have a problem. We see this a lot in our interviews. When we talked with the vice president of HR at an electronics firm, she mentioned the widely publicized "difficulties other corporations are having" and added, "We have not had any of those problems . . . we have gone almost four years without any kind of discrimination complaint!" What's more, lab studies show that protective measures like grievance systems lead people to drop their guard and let bias affect their decisions, because they think company policies will guarantee fairness.

Things don't get better when firms put in formal grievance systems; they get worse. Our quantitative analyses show that the managerial ranks of white women and all minority groups except Hispanic men decline—by 3% to 11%—in the five years after companies adopt them.

Still, most employers feel they need some sort of system to intercept complaints, if only because judges like them. One strategy that is gaining ground is the "flexible" complaint system, which offers not only a formal hearing process but also informal mediation. Since an informal resolution doesn't involve hauling the manager before a disciplinary body, it may reduce retaliation. As we'll show, making managers feel accountable without subjecting them to public rebuke tends to help.

Tools for Getting Managers on Board

If these popular solutions backfire, then what can employers do instead to promote diversity?

A number of companies have gotten consistently positive results with tactics that don't focus on control. They apply three basic principles: engage managers in solving the problem, expose them to people from different groups, and encourage social accountability for change.

Engagement

When someone's beliefs and behavior are out of sync, that person experiences what psychologists call "cognitive dissonance." Experiments show that people have a strong tendency to "correct" dissonance by changing either the beliefs or the behavior. So, if you prompt them to act in ways that support a particular view, their opinions shift toward that view. Ask them to write an essay defending the death penalty, and even the penalty's staunch opponents will come to see some merits. When managers actively help boost diversity in their companies, something similar happens: They begin to think of themselves as diversity champions.

Take *college recruitment programs* targeting women and minorities. Our interviews suggest that managers willingly participate when invited. That's partly because the message is positive: "Help us find a greater variety of promising employees!" And involvement is voluntary: Executives sometimes single out managers they think would be good recruiters, but they don't drag anyone along at gunpoint.

Managers who make college visits say they take their charge seriously. They are determined to come back with strong candidates from underrepresented groups—female engineers, for instance, or African-American management trainees. Cognitive dissonance soon kicks in—and managers who were wishy-washy about diversity become converts.

The effects are striking. Five years after a company implements a college recruitment program targeting female employees, the share of white women, black women, Hispanic women, and Asian-American women in its management rises by about 10%, on average. A program focused on minority recruitment increases the proportion of black male managers by 8% and black female managers by 9%.

Mentoring is another way to engage managers and chip away at their biases. In teaching their protégés the ropes and sponsoring them for key training and assignments, mentors help give their charges the breaks they need to develop and advance. The mentors then come to believe that their protégés merit these opportunities— whether they're white men, women, or minorities. That is cognitive dissonance—"Anyone I sponsor must be deserving"—at work again.

While white men tend to find mentors on their own, women and minorities more often need help from formal programs. One reason, as Georgetown's business school dean David Thomas discovered in his research on mentoring, is that white male executives don't feel comfortable reaching out informally to young women and minority men. Yet they are eager to mentor assigned protégés, and women and minorities are often first to sign up for mentors.

Mentoring programs make companies' managerial echelons significantly more diverse: On average they boost the representation of black, Hispanic, and Asian-American women, and Hispanic and Asian-American men, by 9% to 24%. In industries where plenty of college-educated nonmanagers are eligible to move up, like chemicals and electronics, mentoring programs also increase the ranks of white women and black men by 10% or more.

Only about 15% of firms have special college recruitment programs for women and minorities, and only 10% have mentoring programs. Once organizations try them out, though, the upside becomes clear. Consider how these programs helped Coca-Cola in the wake of a race discrimination suit settled in 2000 for a record $193 million. With guidance from a court-appointed external task force, executives in the North America group got involved in recruitment and mentoring initiatives for professionals and middle managers, working specifically toward measurable goals for minorities. Even top leaders helped to recruit and mentor, and talent-sourcing partners were required to broaden their recruitment efforts. After five years, according to former CEO and chairman Neville Isdell, 80% of all mentees had climbed at least one rung in management. Both individual and group mentoring were open to all races but attracted large numbers of African-Americans (who accounted for 36% of protégés). These changes brought important gains. From 2000 to 2006, African-Americans' representation among salaried employees grew from 19.7% to 23%, and Hispanics' from 5.5% to 6.4%. And while African-Americans and Hispanics respectively made up 12% and 4.9% of professionals and middle managers in 2002, just four years later those figures had risen to 15.5% and 5.9%.

This began a virtuous cycle. Today, Coke looks like a different company. This February, *Atlanta Tribune* magazine profiled 17 African-American women in VP roles and above at Coke, including CFO Kathy Waller.

Contact

Evidence that contact between groups can lessen bias first came to light in an unplanned experiment on the European front during World War II. The U.S. army was still segregated, and only whites served in combat roles. High casualties left General Dwight Eisenhower understaffed, and he asked for black volunteers for combat duty. When Harvard sociologist Samuel Stouffer, on leave at the War Department, surveyed troops on their racial attitudes, he found that whites whose companies had been joined by black platoons showed dramatically lower racial animus and greater willingness to work alongside blacks than those whose companies remained segregated.

Stouffer concluded that whites fighting alongside blacks came to see them as soldiers like themselves first and foremost. The key, for Stouffer, was that whites and blacks had to be working toward a common goal *as equals*—hundreds of years of close contact during and after slavery hadn't dampened bias.

Business practices that generate this kind of contact across groups yield similar results. Take *self-managed teams,* which allow people in different roles and functions to work together on projects as equals. Such teams increase contact among diverse types of people, because specialties within firms are still largely divided along racial, ethnic, and gender lines. For example, women are more likely than men to work in sales, whereas white men are more likely to be in tech jobs and management, and black and Hispanic men are more likely to be in production.

As in Stouffer's combat study, working side-by-side breaks down stereotypes, which leads to more equitable hiring and promotion. At firms that create self-managed work teams, the share of white women, black men and women, and Asian-American women in management rises by 3% to 6% over five years.

Rotating management trainees through departments is another way to increase contact. Typically, this kind of *cross-training* allows people to try their hand at various jobs and deepen their understanding of the whole organization. But it also has a positive impact on diversity, because it exposes both department heads and trainees to a wider variety of people. The result, we've seen, is a bump of 3% to 7% in white women, black men and women, and Asian-American men and women in management.

About a third of U.S. firms have self-managed teams for core operations, and nearly four-fifths use cross-training, so these tools are already available in many organizations. Though college recruitment and mentoring have a bigger impact on diversity—perhaps because they activate engagement in the diversity mission *and* create intergroup contact—every bit helps. Self-managed teams and cross-training have had more positive effects than mandatory diversity training, performance evaluations, job testing, or grievance procedures, which are supposed to promote diversity.

Social accountability

The third tactic, encouraging social accountability, plays on our need to look good in the eyes of those around us. It is nicely illustrated by an experiment conducted in Israel. Teachers in training graded identical compositions attributed to Jewish students with Ashkenazic names (European heritage) or with Sephardic names (African or Asian heritage). Sephardic students typically come from poorer families and do worse in school. On average, the teacher trainees gave the Ashkenazic essays Bs and the Sephardic essays Ds. The difference evaporated, however, when trainees were told that they would discuss their grades with peers. The idea that they might have to explain their decisions led them to judge the work by its quality.

In the workplace you'll see a similar effect. Consider this field study conducted by Emilio Castilla of MIT's Sloan School of Management: A firm found it consistently gave African-Americans smaller raises than whites, even when they had identical job titles and performance ratings. So Castilla suggested transparency to activate social accountability. The firm posted each unit's average performance rating and pay raise by race and gender. Once managers realized that employees, peers, and superiors would know which parts of the company favored whites, the gap in raises all but disappeared.

Corporate *diversity task forces* help promote social accountability. CEOs usually assemble these teams, inviting department heads to volunteer and including members of underrepresented groups. Every quarter or two, task forces look at diversity numbers for the whole company, for business units, and for departments to figure out what needs attention.

After investigating where the problems are—recruitment, career bottlenecks, and so on—task force members come up with solutions, which they then take back to their departments. They notice if their colleagues aren't volunteering to mentor or showing up at recruitment events. Accountability theory suggests that having a task force member in a department will cause managers in it to ask themselves, "Will this look right?" when making hiring and promotion decisions.

Which Diversity Efforts Actually Succeed?

IN 829 MIDSIZE AND LARGE U.S. FIRMS, we analyzed how various diversity initiatives affected the proportion of women and minorities in management. Here you can see which ones helped different groups gain ground—and which set them back, despite good intentions. (No bar means we can't say with statistical certainty if the program had any effect.)

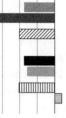

- White men
- White women
- Black men
- Black women
- Hispanic men
- Hispanic women
- Asian men
- Asian women

Poor returns on the usual programs

The three most popular interventions made firms less diverse, not more, because managers resisted strong-arming.

% Change over five years

Mandatory diversity training for managers led to significant decreases for Asian-Americans and black women.

Testing job applicants hurt women and minorities—but not because they perform poorly. Hiring managers don't always test everyone (white men often get a pass) and don't interpret results consistently.

Grievance systems likewise reduced diversity pretty much across the board. Though they're meant to reform biased managers, they often lead to retaliation.

Programs that get results

Companies do a better job of increasing diversity when they forgo the control tactics and frame their efforts more positively. The most effective programs spark engagement, increase contact among different groups, or draw on people's strong desire to look good to others.

Voluntary training doesn't get managers' defenses up the way mandatory training does—and results in increases for several groups.

Self-managed teams aren't designed to improve diversity, but they help by increasing contact between groups, which are often concentrated in certain functions.

Cross-training also increases managers' exposure to people from different groups. Gains for some groups appear to come at a cost to Hispanic men.

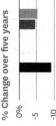

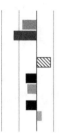

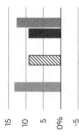

College recruitment targeting women turns recruiting managers into diversity champions, so it also helps boost the numbers for black and Asian-American men.

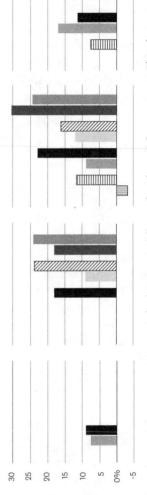

30
25
20
15
10
5
0%
-5

College recruitment targeting minorities often focuses on historically black schools, which lifts the numbers of African-American men and women.

Mentoring has an especially positive impact. Managers who sponsor women and minorities come to believe, through their increased contact, that their protégés deserve the training and opportunities they've received.

Diversity task forces promote social accountability because members bring solutions back to their departments—and notice whether their colleagues adopt them.

Diversity managers sometimes put ineffective programs in place but have a positive impact overall—in part because managers know someone might ask them about their hiring and promotion decisions.

Note: In our analysis, we've isolated the effects of diversity programs from everything else going on in the companies and in the economy.

Deloitte has seen how powerful social accountability can be. In 1992, Mike Cook, who was then the CEO, decided to try to stanch the hemorrhaging of female associates. Half the company's hires were women, but nearly all of them left before they were anywhere near making partner. As Douglas McCracken, CEO of Deloitte's consulting unit at the time, later recounted in HBR, Cook assembled a high-profile task force that "didn't immediately launch a slew of new organizational policies aimed at outlawing bad behavior" but, rather, relied on transparency to get results.

The task force got each office to monitor the career progress of its women and set its own goals to address local problems. When it became clear that the CEO and other managing partners were closely watching, McCracken wrote, "women started getting their share of premier client assignments and informal mentoring." And unit heads all over the country began getting questions from partners and associates about why things weren't changing faster. An external advisory council issued annual progress reports, and individual managers chose change metrics to add to their own performance ratings. In eight years turnover among women dropped to the same level as turnover among men, and the proportion of female partners increased from 5% to 14%—the highest percentage among the big accounting firms. By 2015, 21% of Deloitte's global partners were women, and in March of that year, Deloitte LLP appointed Cathy Engelbert as its CEO—making her the first woman to head a major accountancy.

Task forces are the trifecta of diversity programs. In addition to promoting accountability, they engage members who might have previously been cool to diversity projects and increase contact among the women, minorities, and white men who participate. They pay off, too: On average, companies that put in diversity task forces see 9% to 30% increases in the representation of white women and of each minority group in management over the next five years.

Diversity managers, too, boost inclusion by creating social accountability. To see why, let's go back to the finding of the teacher-in-training experiment, which is supported by many studies: When people know they *might* have to explain their decisions, they are less likely to act on bias. So simply having a diversity manager who could ask them questions prompts managers to step back and consider everyone who is qualified instead of hiring or promoting the first people who come to mind. Companies that appoint diversity managers see 7% to 18% increases in all underrepresented groups—except Hispanic men—in management in the following five years. Those are the gains after accounting for both effective and ineffective programs they put in place.

Only 20% of medium and large employers have task forces, and just 10% have diversity managers, despite the benefits of both. Diversity managers cost money, but task forces use existing workers, so they're a lot cheaper than some of the things that fail, such as mandatory training.

Leading companies like Bank of America Merrill Lynch, Facebook, and Google have placed big bets on accountability in the past couple of years. Expanding on Deloitte's early example, they're now posting complete diversity numbers for all to see. We should know in a few years if that moves the needle for them.

––––––––––

Strategies for controlling bias—which drive most diversity efforts—have failed spectacularly since they were introduced to promote equal opportunity. Black men have barely gained ground in corporate management since 1985. White women haven't progressed since 2000. It isn't that there aren't enough educated women and minorities out there—both groups have made huge educational gains over the past two generations. The problem is that we can't motivate people by forcing them to get with the program and punishing them if they don't.

The numbers sum it up. Your organization will become less diverse, not more, if you require managers to go to diversity training, try to regulate their hiring and promotion decisions, and put in a legalistic grievance system.

The very good news is that we know what does work—we just need to do more of it.

Originally published in July–August 2016. Reprint R1607C

"Numbers Take Us Only So Far"

by Maxine Williams

I WAS ONCE EVICTED FROM an apartment because I was black. I had secured a lovely place on the banks of Lake Geneva through an agent and therefore hadn't met the owner in person before signing the lease. Once my family and I moved in and the color of my skin was clear to see, the landlady asked us to leave. If she had known that I was black, I was told, she would never have rented to me.

Terrible as it felt at the time, her directness was useful to me. It meant I didn't have to scour the facts looking for some other, non-racist rationale for her sudden rejection.

Many people have been denied housing, bank loans, jobs, promotions, and more because of their race. But they're rarely told that's the reason, as I was—particularly in the workplace. For one thing, such discrimination is illegal. For another, executives tend to think—and have a strong desire to believe—that they're hiring and promoting people fairly when they aren't. (Research shows that individuals who view themselves as objective are often the ones who apply the most unconscious bias.) Though managers don't cite or (usually) even perceive race as a factor in their decisions, they use ambiguous assessment criteria to filter out people who aren't like them, research by Kellogg professor Lauren Rivera shows. People in marginalized racial and ethnic groups are deemed more often than whites to be "not the right cultural fit" or "not ready" for high-level roles; they're taken out of the running because their "communication style" is

45

somehow off the mark. They're left only with lingering suspicions that their identity is the real issue, especially when decision makers' bias is masked by good intentions.

I work in the field of diversity. I've also been black my whole life. So I know that underrepresented people in the workplace yearn for two things: The first is to hear that they're not crazy to suspect, at times, that there's a connection between negative treatment and bias. The second is to be offered institutional support.

The first need has a clear path to fulfillment. When we encounter colleagues or friends who have been mistreated and who believe that their identity may be the reason, we should acknowledge that it's fair to be suspicious. There's no leap of faith here—numerous studies show how pervasive such bias still is.

But how can we address the second need? In an effort to find valid, scalable ways to counteract or reverse bias and promote diversity, organizations are turning to people analytics—a relatively new field in business operations and talent management that replaces gut decisions with data-driven practices. People analytics aspires to be "evidence based." And for some HR issues—such as figuring out how many job interviews are needed to assess a candidate, or determining how employees' work commutes affect their job satisfaction—it is. Statistically significant findings have led to some big changes in organizations. Unfortunately, companies that try to apply analytics to the challenges of underrepresented groups at work often complain that the relevant data sets don't include enough people to produce reliable insights—the sample size, the n, is too small. Basically they're saying, "If only there were more of you, we could tell you why there are so few of you."

Companies have access to more data than they realize, however. To supplement a small n, they can venture out and look at the larger context in which they operate. But data volume alone won't give leaders the insight they need to increase diversity in their organizations. They must also take a closer look at the individuals from underrepresented groups who work for them—those who barely register on the analytics radar.

Idea in Brief

Though executives tend to think—and want to believe—they're hiring and promoting fairly, bias still creeps into their decisions. They often use ambiguous criteria to filter out people who aren't like them or deem people from minority groups to be "not the right cultural fit," leaving those employees with the uneasy feeling that their identity might be the real issue.

Companies need to acknowledge that it's fair for employees from underrepresented groups to be suspicious about bias, says Williams, Facebook's global director of diversity. They also must find ways to give those workers more support. To that end, many organizations are turning to people analytics, which aspires to replace gut decisions with data-driven ones. Unfortunately, firms often say that they don't have enough people from marginalized groups in their data sets to produce reliable insights.

But there are things employers can do to supplement small n's: draw on industry or sector data; learn from what's happening in other companies; and deeply examine the experiences of individuals who work for them, talking with them to gather critical qualitative information. If firms are systematic and comprehensive in these efforts, they'll have a better chance of improving diversity and inclusion.

Supplementing the n

Nonprofit research organizations are doing important work that sheds light on how bias shapes hiring and advancement in various industries and sectors. For example, a study by the Ascend Foundation showed that in 2013 white men and white women in five major Silicon Valley firms were 154% more likely to become executives than their Asian counterparts were. And though both race and gender were factors in the glass ceiling for Asians, race had 3.7 times the impact that gender did.

It took two more years of research and analysis—using data on several hundred thousand employees, drawn from the EEOC's aggregation of all Bay Area technology firms and from the individual reports of 13 U.S. tech companies—before Ascend determined how bias affected the prospects of blacks and Hispanics. Among those groups it again found that, overall, race had a greater negative impact

Asian Americans Are the Least Likely Group in the U.S. to Be Promoted to Management

by Buck Gee and Denise Peck

Asian Americans are the forgotten minority in the glass-ceiling conversation.

This was painfully obvious to us as we read the newly released diversity and inclusion report from a large Silicon Valley company: Its 19 pages never specifically address Asian Americans. Asian men are lumped into a "non-underrepresented" category with white men, and Asian women are assigned to a category that includes women of all races. In contrast, the report addresses Hispanics, African Americans, and Native Americans as distinct categories. Ironically, the chief diversity and inclusion officer of the company remarked about its efforts, "If you do not intentionally include, you will unintentionally exclude."

But excluded from the report is the fact that Asian Americans are the least likely racial group to be promoted into Silicon Valley's management and executive levels, even though they are the most likely to be hired into high-tech jobs. This was a key finding in a 2017 report we coauthored for the Ascend Foundation ("The Illusion of Asian Success"), analyzing EEOC data on Silicon Valley's management pipeline.

Across the country, the results are the same. Our analysis of national EEOC workforce data found that Asian American white-collar professionals are the least likely group to be promoted from individual contributor roles into management—less likely than any other race, including blacks and Hispanics. And our analysis found that white professionals are about twice as likely to be promoted into management as their Asian American counterparts.

It's easy to understand why Asian American representation in the workforce may not seem to be an issue. In some key measures, Asian Americans are the most successful U.S. demographic—more highly educated, for example, and with higher median incomes than any other racial group, according to the Pew Research Center. More significant, Asian Americans make up 12% of the professional workforce even though they form only 5.6% of the U.S. population. This fact underlies the potential blind spot for many companies: Because Asian Americans are not considered an underrepresented minority, they are given little priority or attention in diversity programs. We have found that in many companies throughout the country, Asian-related programs are geared toward cultural inclusion, not management diversity.

When we were tech executives in Silicon Valley, our corporate responsibility was to grow the business by building a highly skilled and motivated workforce through hiring, developing, and promoting the best talent. The large numbers of Asian Americans in the professional workforce confirm that businesses are finding qualified Asian Americans to hire. However, the disparity in numbers between the lower ranks and the executive levels suggests either that leadership potential is disproportionately lacking in Asian Americans or—much more likely—that companies have not done an adequate job of identifying and developing Asian American talent.

These issues aren't confined to the tech industry. Similar concerns were raised about the legal profession in a 2017 study coauthored by Goodwin Liu, associate justice of the California Supreme Court. Published by Yale Law School and the National Asian Pacific American Bar Association, the report found that Asian Americans are well represented in law—they constitute more than 10% of the graduates of the top 30 law schools—yet "have the highest attrition rates and lowest ratio of partners to associates among all [racial] groups."

A similar finding with New York banks was reported in *Bloomberg Businessweek* last year. As one example, Goldman Sachs reported that 27% of its U.S. professional workforce was Asian American, but only 11% of its U.S. executives and senior managers, and none of its executive officers, were.

The list of industries goes on. The Ascend Foundation, the pan-Asian organization that published our 2017 paper, was established by a group of pan-Asian accounting partners. They had found that while over 20% of the associates in many of the larger accounting firms were Asian American, very few were being promoted to the partner level.

And this problem is not limited to private industry: While Asian Americans made up 9.8% of the federal professional workforce in 2016, they represented only 4.4% of the workforce at the highest federal level.

Buck Gee is a former Silicon Valley executive and a member of the Committee of 100. He received his BS/MSEE from Stanford University and his MBA from Harvard Business School. **Denise Peck** is a former executive at Cisco Systems and Sun Microsystems and is currently an Executive Advisor at the Ascend Foundation. She received her BA from the University of California, Berkeley, and her MBA from Stanford University.

Originally published in May 2018. Reprint H04D81

than gender on advancement from the professional to the executive level. In the Bay Area white women fared worse than white men but much better than all Asians, Hispanics, and blacks. Minority women faced the biggest obstacle to entering the executive ranks. Black and Hispanic women were severely challenged by both their low numbers at the professional level and their lower chances of rising from professional to executive. Asian women, who had more representation at the professional level than other minorities, had the lowest chances of moving up from professional to executive. An analysis of national data found similar results.

By analyzing industry or sector data on underrepresented groups—and examining patterns in hiring, promotions, and other decisions about talent—we can better manage the problems and risks in our own organizations. Tech companies may look at the Ascend reports and say, "Hey, let's think about what's happening with our competitors' talent. There's a good chance it's happening here, too." Their HR teams might then add a layer of career tracking for women of color, for example, or create training programs for managing diverse teams.

Another approach is to extrapolate lessons from other companies' analyses. We might look, for instance, at Red Ventures, a Charlotte-based digital media company. Red Ventures is diverse by several measures. (It has a Latino CEO, and about 40% of its employees are people of color.) But that doesn't mean there aren't problems to solve. When I met with its top executives, they told me they had recently done an analysis of performance reviews at the firm and found that internalized stereotypes were having a negative effect on black and Latino employees' self-assessments. On average, members of those two groups rated their performance 30% lower than their managers did (whereas white male employees scored their performance 10% higher than their managers did). The study also uncovered a correlation between racial isolation and negative self-perception. For example, people of color who worked in engineering generally rated themselves lower than those who worked in sales, where there were more blacks and Latinos. These patterns were consistent at all levels, from junior to senior staff.

In response, the HR team at Red Ventures trained employees in how to do self-assessments, and that has started to close the gap for blacks and Latinos (who more recently rated themselves 22% lower than their managers did). Hallie Cornetta, the company's VP of human capital, explained that the training "focused on the importance of completing quantitative and qualitative self-assessments honestly, in a way that shows how employees personally view their performance across our five key dimensions, rather than how they assume their manager or peers view their performance." She added: "We then shared tangible examples of what 'exceptional' versus 'solid' versus 'needs improvement' looks like in these dimensions to remove some of the subjectivity and help minority—and all—employees assess with greater direction and confidence."

Getting Personal

Once we've gone broader by supplementing the n, we can go deeper by examining individual cases. This is critical. Algorithms and statistics do not capture what it feels like to be the only black or Hispanic team member or the effect that marginalization has on individual employees and the group as a whole. We must talk openly with people, one-on-one, to learn about their experiences with bias, and share our own stories to build trust and make the topic safe for discussion. What we discover through those conversations is every bit as important as what shows up in the aggregated data.

An industry colleague, who served as a lead on diversity at a tech company, broke it down for me like this: "When we do our employee surveys, the Latinos always say they are happy. But I'm Latino, and I know that we are often hesitant to rock the boat. Saying the truth is too risky, so we'll say what you want to hear—even if you sit us down in a focus group. I also know that those aggregated numbers where there are enough of us for the n to be significant don't reflect the heterogeneity in our community. Someone who is light-skinned and grew up in Latin America in an upper-middle-class family probably is very happy and comfortable indeed. Someone who is darker-skinned and grew up working-class in America is probably not feeling that same sense of belonging. I'm going to spend time and effort trying to build solutions for the ones I know are at a disadvantage, whether the data tells me that there's a problem with all Latinos or not."

This is a recurring theme. I spoke with 10 diversity and HR professionals at companies with head counts ranging from 60 to 300,000, all of whom are working on programs or interventions for the people who don't register as "big" in big data. They rely at least somewhat on their own intuition when exploring the impact of marginalization. This may seem counter to the mission of people analytics, which is to remove personal perspective and gut feelings from the talent equation entirely. But to discover the effects of bias in our organizations—and to identify complicating factors within groups, such as class and colorism among Latinos and others—we need to collect and analyze qualitative data, too. Intuition can help us find it. The diversity and HR folks described using their "spidey sense" or knowing there is "something in the water"—essentially, understanding that bias is probably a factor, even though people analytics doesn't always prove causes and predict outcomes. Through conversations with employees—and sometimes through focus groups, if the resources are there and participants feel it's safe to be honest—they reality-check what their instincts tell them, often drawing on their own experiences with bias. One colleague said, "The combination of qualitative and quantitative data is ideal, but at the end of the day there is nothing that data will tell us that we don't already know as black people. I know what my experience was as an African-American man who worked for 16 years in roles that weren't related to improving diversity. It's as much heart as head in this work."

A Call to Action

The proposition at the heart of people analytics is sound—if you want to hire and manage fairly, gut-based decisions are not enough. However, we have to create a new approach, one that also works for small data sets—for the marginalized and the underrepresented.

Here are my recommendations:

First, analysts must challenge the traditional minimum confident n, pushing themselves to look beyond the limited hard data. They don't have to prove that the difference in performance ratings between blacks and whites is "statistically significant" to help managers understand the impact of bias in performance reviews. We already know from the breadth and depth of social science research about bias that it is pervasive in the workplace and influences ratings, so we can combine those insights with what we hear and see on the ground and simply start operating as if bias exists in our companies. We may have to place a higher value on the experiences shared by five or 10 employees—or look more carefully at the descriptive data, such as head counts for underrepresented groups and average job satisfaction scores cut by race and gender—to examine the impact of bias at a more granular level.

In addition, analysts should frequently provide confidence intervals—that is, guidance on how much managers can trust the data if the n's are too small to prove statistical significance. When managers get that information, they're more likely to make changes in their hiring and management practices, even if they believe—as most do—that they are already treating people fairly. Suppose, for example, that as Red Ventures began collecting data on self-assessments, analysts had a 75% confidence level that blacks and Latinos were underrating themselves. The analysts could then have advised managers to go to their minority direct reports, examine the results from that performance period, and determine together whether the self-reviews truly reflected their contributions. It's a simple but collaborative way to address implicit bias or stereotyping that you're reasonably sure is there while giving agency to each employee.

Second, companies also need to be more consistent and comprehensive in their qualitative analysis. Many already conduct interviews and focus groups to gain insights on the challenges of the underrepresented; some even do textual analysis of written performance reviews, exit interview notes, and hiring memos, looking for language that signals bias or negative stereotyping. But we have to go further. We need to find a viable way to create and process more-objective performance evaluations, given the internalized biases of both employees and managers, and to determine how those biases affect ratings.

This journey begins with educating all employees on the real-life impact of bias and negative stereotypes. At Facebook we offer a variety of training programs with an emphasis on spotting and counteracting bias, and we keep reinforcing key messages post-training, since we know these muscles take time to build. We issue reminders at critical points to shape decision making and behavior. For example, in our performance evaluation tool, we incorporate prompts for people to check word choice when writing reviews and self-assessments. We remind them, for instance, that terms like "cultural fit" can allow bias to creep in and that they should avoid describing women as "bossy" if they wouldn't describe men who demonstrated the same behaviors that way. We don't yet have data on how this is influencing the language used—it's a new intervention—but we will be examining patterns over time.

Perhaps above all, HR and analytics departments must value both qualitative and quantitative expertise and apply mixed-method approaches everywhere possible. At Facebook we're building cross-functional teams with both types of specialists, because no single research method can fully capture the complex layers of bias that everyone brings to the workplace. We view all research methods as trying to solve the same problem from different angles. Sometimes we approach challenges from a quantitative perspective first, to uncover the "what" before looking to the qualitative experts to dive into the "why" and "how." For instance, if the numbers showed that certain teams were losing or attracting minority employees at higher rates than others (the "what"), we might conduct interviews, run focus groups, or analyze text from company surveys to understand the "why," and pull out themes or lessons for other parts of the company. In other scenarios we might reverse the order of those steps. For example, if we repeatedly heard from members of one social group that they weren't seeing their peers getting recognized at the same rate as people in other groups, we could then investigate whether numerical trends confirmed those observations, or conduct statistical analyses to figure out which organizational circumstances were associated with employees' being more or less likely to get recognized.

Cross-functional teams also help us reap the benefits of cognitive diversity. Working together stretches everyone, challenging team members' own assumptions and biases. Getting to absolute "whys" and "hows" on any issue, from recruitment to engagement to performance, is always going to be tough. But we believe that with this approach, we stand the best chance of making improvements across the company. As we analyze the results of Facebook's Pulse survey, given twice a year to employees, and review Performance Summary Cycle inputs, we'll continue to look for signs of problems as well as progress.

Evidence of discrimination or unfair outcomes may not be as certain or obvious in the workplace as it was for me the time I was evicted from my apartment. But we can increase our certainty, and it's essential that we do so. The underrepresented people at our companies are not crazy to perceive biases working against them, and they can get institutional support.

Originally published in November–December 2017. Reprint R1706L

Race Matters

The Truth About Mentoring Minorities.
by David A. Thomas

DIVERSITY HAS BECOME A TOP priority in corporate America. Despite the best intentions, though, many organizations have failed to achieve racial balance within their executive teams. Some have revolving doors for talented minorities, recruiting the best and brightest only to see them leave, frustrated and even angered by the barriers they encounter. Other companies are able to retain high-potential professionals of color only to have them become mired in middle management. Still others have minorities in their executive ranks, but only in racialized positions, such as those dealing with community relations, equal employment opportunity, or ethnic markets.

In my research on the career progression of minorities at U.S. corporations, I have found that whites and minorities follow distinct patterns of advancement. Specifically, promising white professionals tend to enter a fast track early in their careers, whereas high-potential minorities take off much later, typically after they have reached middle management. I've also found that the people of color who advance the furthest all share one characteristic—a strong network of mentors and corporate sponsors who nurture their professional development.

These findings have key implications for mentors—mainly that to be effective, they must fully appreciate all the developmental roles they play (such as that of coach, advocate, and counselor) and understand the importance of each at different stages of their protégé's career. The mentor of a professional of color must also be aware of

About the Research

MY THREE-YEAR RESEARCH PROJECT took place at three major U.S. corporations: a manufacturer of commodity products, an electronics company, and a high-tech firm. At these multibillion-dollar organizations, I conducted in-depth case studies of 20 minority executives, predominantly African-Americans but also Asian- and Hispanic-Americans. For comparison purposes, I also conducted in-depth studies of 13 white executives as well as 21 nonexecutives (people who had plateaued in middle management), both white and minority, from the same companies. In addition, I reviewed the promotion records of more than 500 managers and executives at one of the companies studied.

Each corporation in the study had a long history of commitment to diversity. Amid the civil rights environment of the 1960s and early 1970s, all had strongly supported both affirmative action and equal employment opportunities. Their civic and community involvement helped their initial efforts to recruit minorities for professional and managerial positions. By the early 1990s, these companies had achieved racial integration within their management ranks.

Some people have questioned my decision to study only companies with a good track record in terms of diversity. The reason is simple: I felt that these companies would have more to teach us about how minority executives could succeed—even given various obstacles. I do not, however, mean to gloss over the very real—and sometimes insurmountable—barriers that many nonwhites face in their quest for advancement in corporate America. Indeed, there are still many companies at which no amount of individual effort, preparation, or performance is likely to propel a person of color into an executive position.

---

the challenges race can present to his protégé's career development and advancement. Only then can the mentor help his protégé build a network of relationships with people who can pave the way to the executive level. As a foundation, then, mentors must first understand how people of color tend to climb the corporate ladder.

Patterns of Movement

In a three-year research project, I studied the career trajectories of minority and white professionals at three major U.S. corporations. The story of one of the participants—Stephen Williams—sheds light on many of the differences in career advancement between whites and minorities. (In the interest of privacy, I have used pseudonyms

Idea in Brief

You've hired the best and brightest—only to watch many promising *minority* professionals get mired in middle management and leave, frustrated and angry, for better careers with your competitors.

Why the exodus? It's the **two-tournament system:** According to a recent study, whites tend to fast track early; minorities, after years in middle management. Minority managers who stay motivated during the protracted early stages of their careers—and finally reach the executive level—share a key resource: a strong network of mentors and corporate sponsors who provide instruction, coaching, and—most important—long-term, close developmental support.

The two-tournament system isn't fair. But until it's eradicated, minorities can best advance by building and drawing on a solid mentoring network. They *and* their companies win.

for the participants. For additional details about the study, see the sidebar "About the Research.")

Williams, an African-American, was born and raised in a middle-class neighborhood in Washington, DC. After earning his bachelor's degree at one of the nation's leading colleges, he began his career as a design engineer at a multibillion-dollar electronics corporation. On his first day in the lab there, he encountered a large banner that read, "George Wallace for President." That proclamation for the pro-segregationist former governor of Alabama was an omen of the uphill battle Williams faced. And yet Williams eventually reached the executive level at his organization. Why did he make it when so many other minorities plateaued in middle management?

First, Williams had the good fortune to be hired by Nathan Barrett, a white manager who continually expanded Williams's responsibilities and advised him on office politics. By the end of his early career, Williams had won additional supporters within the company, including Barrett's boss and several white peers who, when they were promoted to management before Williams, vouched for him with their colleagues and recruited him for plum assignments.

Although it took Williams longer to reach middle management than he thought it should, he avoided becoming cynical even as

Idea in Practice

The stark difference in career trajectories of white and minority executives has major implications for high-potential minorities—and their mentors—during each career-development stage:

Stage 1: Entry Level to Middle Management

As minorities watch their white counterparts quickly receive plum assignments and promotions into middle management, many grow discouraged. But *some* remain motivated. How? They forge mentoring relationships with widely diverse individuals who open the door to challenging assignments and expanded responsibilities, sending the message, "These are high performers." Mentors also provide career advice and protect protégés from people leveling unfair criticism.

Result? During this stage, future minority executives evaluate themselves in terms of personal growth, not external rewards. Less concerned with how slowly they're climbing the corporate ladder, they embrace the work itself.

Stage 2: Middle to Upper Middle Management

Promising minorities "catch up" to fast-tracked whites. Through promotions, they deepen and broaden their functional expertise, gaining influence over subordinates who might otherwise be resistant to minority leaders.

Tackling more complex challenges, minorities demonstrate their potential and extend their credibility. By changing functions, requesting special projects, and switching locations, they further enhance their success. At this stage, they extend their mentoring relationships to include powerful corporate-level sponsors.

his white peers were being promoted. Instead, he concentrated on strengthening his technical proficiency, taking numerous in-house courses and seminars. He also chose his assignments judiciously, consciously avoiding being sidetracked into nontechnical or support jobs. Throughout this period, he earned the reputation for being an excellent performer, and he gained the cooperation, respect, and sometimes the friendship of whites who were initially either resistant or hesitant to work with him. After seven years as an engineer, Williams decided to pursue his MBA while continuing to work in engineering and design assignments. The education facilitated his transition into management when he was finally promoted two years later.

Once in middle management, Williams's career took off; he was charged with coordinating the engineering, manufacturing, and

Stage 3: Upper Middle to Executive Level

Minority and white executives finally converge. Minority managers take on challenges specific to working cross-functionally, learning to think and act more strategically and politically. To further distinguish themselves, they score highly visible successes directly related to the company's core strategy.

They also continue developing their networks of highly placed mentors and sponsors. Their relationships with their immediate bosses become particularly crucial. They establish several new, long-term relationships with other executives as well, both white and minority.

Cross-Race Mentoring Challenges

Cross-race mentoring relationships raise unique challenges. For example, some minority protégés may avoid such relationships so as not to attract scrutiny, spawn peers' resentment, or "sell out" their culture.

But if both parties can build a strong foundation of mutual trust, they'll more likely surmount those challenges. If you're a mentor:

- Openly discuss racial sensitivities. Minorities tend to advance further when their white mentors acknowledge race as a potential barrier.

- See yourself in your protégés— they're like you were, years ago. If you can identify with each other, you'll forge closer relationships.

- If you're unsure whether you're the best role model, help protégés identify other appropriate supporters.

field service for ensuring the quality of what was to become a major product family. His success in that position propelled him to a series of other assignments, including a temporary one in strategic planning, that eventually landed him a promotion to vice president and general manager, with profit-and-loss responsibility for a major business unit.

Williams's experiences were typical of the minority executives in my study, which tracked the various stages of career development. Stage 1 covered entry level to middle management. Stage 2 included middle management to upper middle management. (A person in Stage 2 supervised other managers and had responsibility for a functional department within a business unit—for example, the director of marketing or a plant manager.) And Stage 3 covered upper middle management to the executive level. (A person in this stage became a corporate officer or a direct report of a corporate officer, with responsibility for an integrated business unit—a division president, for instance—or leadership of a corporate function—such as a vice president of purchasing.)

The most striking aspect of my findings was the consistency of the data. (See the exhibit "Separate and unequal.") White professionals who eventually became executives—a group I'll henceforth refer to simply as "white executives"—usually entered a fast track in Stage 1, whereas both white and minority professionals who later plateaued in middle management and minorities who eventually became executives all inched along during that period. In Stages 2 and 3, the careers of minorities who ultimately became executives took off, surpassing those of the plateaued managers. This stark difference in the career trajectories of white and minority executives suggests that companies implicitly have two distinct tournaments for access to the top jobs. In the tournament for whites, contenders are sorted early on, and only those deemed most promising proceed to future competition. In the tournament for minorities, the screening process for the best jobs occurs much later. This and other differences have important implications for minority professionals—and for the people mentoring them through the different stages.

Stage 1

According to my research, a pernicious result of the two-tournament system was that many high-potential minorities became discouraged when they failed to be fast-tracked early in their careers. They became demotivated—especially when they saw their white colleagues receive plum assignments and promotions—and deskilled. As a result, their performance fell to a level that matched their modest rewards.

But some minorities—those who eventually became executives—avoided that fate. What kept them motivated and prepared to take advantage of opportunities that arrived belatedly? A common thread among them was their relationships with mentors. Even though the minority executives were not on an obvious fast track,

Separate and unequal

White and minority executives do not progress up the corporate ladder in the same way. Early in their careers, high-potential whites enter a fast track, arriving in middle management well before their peers. Promising professionals of color, on the other hand, break through much later, usually after their arrival in middle management. These data are for a multibillion-dollar manufacturer of commodity products; studies at two other large U.S. corporations have shown similar results.

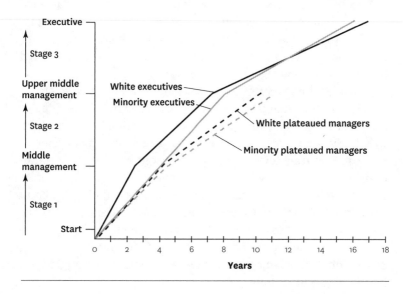

influential mentors were investing in them as if they were, which helped prevent them from either ratcheting down their performance or simply leaving the organization.

This is not to say that the minorities in the study who became executives didn't experience their share of disappointments; they did. But they evaluated themselves in terms of personal growth, not external rewards. Committed to excellence, they found the process of learning new skills rewarding. Like Williams, many of them went to graduate school or took training courses to enhance their knowledge. In general, minority executives made early career choices that placed them at the leading edge of the work they liked. They were more enthusiastic about the work itself and less concerned with how quickly—or slowly—they were climbing the corporate ladder. In fact, two minority executives in the study actually took demotions to transfer from staff jobs into operations, where they saw a better match for their skills and a greater opportunity for professional growth. Stage 1 was thus a time for minority executives to gain the three C's: confidence, competence, and credibility.

In contrast, minority professionals who subsequently plateaued in middle management tended to make their decisions based on perceived fast-track career opportunities, not on the actual work. They were more prone to take salary and title promotions that offered little increase in management responsibility.

Consider the career of Roosevelt James, a minority electrical engineer at the same company as Stephen Williams. While Williams was focused on engineering and design early in his career, James was motivated more by the prospect of getting into management. He took one transfer after another, accepting nominal promotions, believing they were stepping stones to a larger goal. Before reaching middle management, he had had a total of 12 different assignments (nearly all lateral moves) in seven different functional areas, including those in facilities management and affirmative action. Ironically, to fulfill their ambitions for upward mobility, professionals like James sometimes left the path that might have led to the executive suite.

Interestingly, minority executives were promoted to middle management only slightly faster than minority plateaued managers, but with much greater job continuity. They were much less likely to have changed departments, made lateral moves, or transferred away from core positions. Surprisingly, they even received, on average, fewer promotions within a given level than did minorities who failed to make it past middle management. A close inspection of the data, however, revealed that the promotions of minority managers like James offered little real expansion of responsibilities, as compared with the promotions of minority executives like Williams.

Minority executives attributed much of their later success to their immediate bosses, other superiors, and peers who helped them develop professionally. Of course, such developmental relationships are important for everybody climbing the corporate ladder, regardless of race, but what distinguished minority executives from white executives and plateaued managers was that they had many more such relationships and with a broader range of people, especially in the early years of their careers. Within the first three years at the organization, minority executives had established at least one developmental relationship, usually with a boss or a boss's boss. These mentors provided critical support in five ways.

First, the relationships opened the door to challenging assignments that allowed the minority executives to gain professional competence. Second, by putting the future executives in high-trust positions, the mentors sent a message to the rest of the organization that these people were high performers, thus helping them to gain confidence and establish their credibility. Third, the mentors provided crucial career advice and counsel that prevented their protégés from getting sidetracked from the path leading to the executive level. Fourth, the mentors often became powerful sponsors later in the minority executives' careers, recruiting them repeatedly to new positions. Fifth, the mentors often protected their protégés by confronting subordinates or peers who leveled unfair criticism, especially if it had racial undertones. For example, a superior-performing African-American in the study had a laid-back style that detractors said was an indication of his slacking off, playing on the stereotype that blacks are lazy. The mentor directly challenged the detractors by pointing out that his protégé was the leading salesperson in the division.

Such rich mentoring relationships enabled minority executives to build on the three C's, despite temptations to become discouraged. It took Williams, for instance, nine years to reach middle management, whereas it took his white counterparts roughly five. In contrast, professionals of color who plateaued in middle management tended to have circumscribed relationships with their mentors, often limited to work-related issues.

In summary, in Stage 1, the winners in the white tournament earned fast promotions into middle management. In the minority tournament, the signals sent to winners were more subtle, taking the form of rich mentoring relationships, challenging assignments, and expanded responsibilities, which showed the rest of the organization that these people merited future investment. (Winners of the white tournament also received those benefits, but the most obvious prizes in that contest were fast promotions.)

Stage 2

Once minority executives entered middle management, they typically had to wait another ten to 15 years before reaching the executive level. But Stage 2 was usually where their careers took off. And without exception, the minority executives in the study vividly re-called that their initial middle-management jobs were critical to their eventual success. Interestingly, few of the white executives felt that way, perhaps because they didn't regard their jobs in early Stage 2 as big opportunities to prove themselves in the same way that their minority counterparts did.

In Stage 2, minority executives continued to increase their functional knowledge, allowing them to deepen and broaden their foundation of the three C's. When leading others, the sheer technical or functional competence they had acquired in Stage 1 often enabled them to influence subordinates who might otherwise have been resistant. Through that process, they were able to enhance their managerial skills and judgment.

Stage 2 was also an important period for the minority executives to apply their existing skills to complex situations, which then helped them to demonstrate their potential and extend their credibility within the larger organization. Because of that, they were able to expand their network of relationships, including those with mentors and sponsors, beyond the boundaries of their original functional groups. Williams, for example, received several assignments in Stage 2 that required him to develop working relationships with key people in other functional areas. By the end of Stage 2, every minority executive in the study had at least one influential executive as a mentor, and many were highly regarded by several executives who acted as sponsors.

The split between minority executives and plateaued managers became more pronounced in Stage 2. Minority executives still received fewer promotions than minority plateaued managers, but they reached upper middle management in less time because their promotions were bigger and more significant. The assignment patterns of the minority managers continued to be unfocused: they had more job changes—either by department, location, or function (especially changes from line to staff jobs)—and they tended to serve in fix-it roles involving the same kind of challenges over and over, with no opportunity to acquire new skills.

The career of Carlos Amado, one of the managers studied, is a case in point. By the end of Stage 1, Amado had acquired a deep expertise in manufacturing. He had also earned a reputation for turning around problem groups and making them into stars. But in Stage 2, he failed to learn other important skills, such as developing the supervisors who reported to him and delegating work, and his career subsequently stagnated. A lack of savvy mentoring probably contributed to Amado's incomplete understanding that he was being boxed into a limited role.

Stage 2 was also when the careers of minority and white executives began to converge—their experiences, assignments, and pace of advancement became increasingly similar. There were still, however, some notable differences. Compared with their white counterparts, minority executives were twice as likely to change functions, twice as likely to take on special projects or task-force assignments, three times as likely to take a turnaround assignment, almost twice as likely to change locations, and four times as likely to report a big success. In many ways, these differences are a reversal of what occurred in Stage 1, where white executives had markedly more opportunities to prove themselves than minority executives did. For that reason, Stage 2 can be thought of as a catching-up and breaking-out period for minority executives.

Interestingly, although minority and white executives had a similar number of developmental relationships in Stage 2, minority executives were far more likely to have powerful corporate-level executives as sponsors and mentors. In reviewing their careers, minority executives usually described a senior person who had been watching their progress during this period without their full awareness.

Stage 3

The climb from upper middle management to the executive level required a broad base of experience—well beyond a functional expertise. In Stage 3, people took on issues specific to working across functional boundaries, and that change encouraged them to think and act more strategically and politically.

To distinguish oneself as executive-level material in Stage 3, an individual needed highly visible successes that were directly related to the company's core strategy. For Stephen Williams, it was his critical role in developing and launching a product line that helped to reposition his company in the marketplace.

Minority executives in Stage 3 continued developing their network of highly placed mentors and sponsors. An individual's relationship with his executive boss, in particular, became crucial; it played a central role in helping each minority executive break through to the highest level. Furthermore, in Stage 3 the minority executives reported developing at least two new relationships with other executives. In contrast, most of the minority plateaued managers did not establish any new developmental relationships during that time.

The networks of minority executives were also much more diverse than those of the minority managers. For example, African-American managers who plateaued either relied almost exclusively on members of their own racial group for key developmental support or they relied predominantly on whites. In contrast, those who reached the executive level, especially the most successful among them, had built genuine, personal long-term relationships with both whites and African-Americans.

The careers of minority and white executives continued to converge in Stage 3, especially with regard to developmental relationships.

Clearly, it was impossible to make it to the executive level, regardless of race, without the active advocacy of an immediate boss and at least one other key sponsor or mentor. Nevertheless, as was the case in Stage 2, minority executives tended to have a higher proportion of their developmental relationships with the corporate elite than did white executives.

In summary, during Stages 2 and 3, the careers of minority executives became clearly differentiated from that of plateaued managers, and in Stage 3, the career trajectories and experiences of minority and white executives finally converged.

Mentoring Challenges

A key finding of this research is that professionals of color who plateaued in management received mentoring that was basically instructional; it helped them develop better skills. Minority executives, by contrast, enjoyed closer, fuller developmental relationships with their mentors. This was particularly true in people's early careers, when they needed to build confidence, credibility, and competence. That is, purely instructional mentoring was not sufficient; protégés needed to feel connected to their mentors.

Specifically, a mentor must play the dual role of coach and counselor: coaches give technical advice—explaining how to do something—while counselors talk about the experience of doing it and offer emotional support. Both are crucial. If a protégé doesn't have someone to talk to about his experiences in the organization, he will often have trouble implementing any coaching advice. This is especially true early in a person's career, when the instructional advice requires him to assume behaviors that he is not yet comfortable with. Later in the protégé's career, particularly in Stages 2 and 3, the mentor must focus on establishing and expanding a network of relationships, including sponsorship and connections to people who are higher in the organization. While the quality of the interpersonal relationships remains important, the diversity of the network becomes another crucial factor.

Many people, however, do not approach mentoring from a developmental perspective. They don't understand how to work with subordinates, especially minorities, to prepare them for future opportunities. My own experience and the findings of other studies suggest that organizations can change this by educating managers about their developmental role and by teaching them how to mentor effectively. Of prime importance is an understanding of the kinds of developmental relationships that people need at different points in their careers. Also crucial is an appreciation that, because race and racism can pose significant obstacles for people of color, mentors of minorities may need to approach mentoring differently than they do with their white protégés.

Cross-race issues

This education process must include an awareness of the inherent difficulties of mentoring across race. A significant amount of research shows that cross-race (as well as cross-gender) relationships can have difficulty forming, developing, and maturing. Nevertheless, the mentoring of minority professionals must often be across race, as it was for most of the minority executives in my study. And to develop the personal connections that are the foundation of a good mentoring relationship, the participants must overcome the following potential obstacles.

Negative stereotypes. Mentors must be willing to give their protégés the benefit of the doubt: they invest in their protégés because they expect them to succeed. But a potential mentor who holds negative stereotypes about an individual, perhaps based on race, might withhold that support until the prospective protégé has proven herself worthy of investment. (Such subtle racism may help explain why none of the minority professionals in my study had been fast-tracked. Whites were placed on the fast track based on their perceived potential, whereas people of color had to display a proven and sustained record of solid performance—in effect, they often had to be overprepared—before they were placed on the executive track.)

On the other hand, when a person of color feels that he won't be given the benefit of the doubt, he behaves in certain ways—for example, he might not take risks he should for fear that if he fails, he will be punished disproportionately.

Identification and role modeling. Close mentoring relationships are much more likely to form when both parties see parts of themselves in the other person: the protégé sees someone whom he wants to be like in the future. The mentor sees someone who reminds him of himself years ago. This identification process can help the mentor see beyond a protégé's rough edges. But if the mentor has trouble identifying with his protégé—and sometimes differences in race are an obstacle—then he might not be able to see beyond the protégé's weaknesses. Furthermore, when the mentoring relationship is across race, the mentor will often have certain limitations as a role model. That is, if the protégé adopts the behavior of the mentor, it might produce different results. In my study, an African-American participant recounted how his white mentor encouraged him to adopt the mentor's more aggressive style. But when the protégé did so, others labeled him an "angry black man."

Skepticism about intimacy. At companies without a solid track history of diversity, people might question whether close, high-quality relationships across race are possible. Does the mentor, for example, have an ulterior motive, or is the protégé selling out his culture?

Public scrutiny. Because cross-race relationships are rare in most organizations, they tend to be more noticeable, so people focus on them. The possibility of such scrutiny will often discourage people from participating in a cross-race relationship in the first place.

Peer resentment. A protégé's peers can easily become jealous, prompting them to suggest or imply that the protégé does not deserve whatever benefits he's received. Someone who fears such resentment might avoid forming a close relationship with a prospective mentor of another race. Of course, peer resentment occurs even with same-race mentorships, but it is a much greater concern in cross-race relationships because of their rarity.

Such obstacles often hinder cross-race mentoring from reaching its full potential. In my research, I have found that they make people less willing to open up about sensitive issues and more afraid of disagreements and confrontations. The general sense is that cross-race relationships are more fragile.

71

Not surprisingly, many cross-race mentoring relationships suffer from "protective hesitation": both parties refrain from raising touchy issues. For example, Richard Davis, a white mentor in my study, thought that his African-American protégé's style was abrasive, but he kept that feeling to himself in order to avoid any suggestion that he was prejudiced—specifically that he harbored the stereotype that all black men are brash and unpolished. Davis eventually found out that he was right when his protégé's style became an issue with others. At that point, though, his protégé was deemed to have a problem—one that could have been prevented had Davis only spoken sooner.

Protective hesitation can become acute when the issue is race—a taboo topic for many mentors and protégés. People believe that they aren't supposed to talk about race; if they have to discuss it, then it must be a problem. But that mind-set can cripple a relationship. Consider, for example, a protégé who thinks that a client is giving him a difficult time because of his race but keeps his opinion to himself for fear that his mentor will think he has a chip on his shoulder. Had the protégé raised the issue, his mentor might have been able to nip the problem early on. The mentor, for instance, might have sent the protégé to important client meetings alone, thereby signaling that the protégé has the backing of his mentor and the authority to make high-level decisions.

The above example highlights an important finding from my research: minorities tend to advance further when their white mentors understand and acknowledge race as a potential barrier. Then they can help their protégés deal effectively with some of those obstacles. In other words, relationships in which protégé and mentor openly discuss racial issues generally translate into greater opportunity for the protégé.

To encourage and foster that type of mentoring, organizations can teach people, especially managers, how to identify and surmount various race-related difficulties. For example, a white mentor might make a concerted effort to communicate to her minority protégé that she has already given him the benefit of the doubt. In a meeting, she could openly endorse his good ideas, thereby signaling to others that they, too, should value his opinions. Such actions would curb the protégé's fear of failure and encourage him to take risks and speak about difficulties.

And consider the practice of role modeling. If a mentor accepts that he might be limited in his ability to serve as a role model, he can help his protégé identify other appropriate people. He can also offer open-ended advice, perhaps by using qualifying comments ("This might not work for you, but from my experience . . .") and invite discussion of the advice rather than assume it will be taken. Otherwise, the mentor might easily misconstrue situations when his advice isn't taken, which could make the mentor feel slighted and possibly even cause him to abandon the relationship.

It should be noted that when the complexities of cross-race relationships are handled well, they can strengthen a relationship. For one thing, if a mentor and protégé trust each other enough to work together in dealing with touchy race-related issues, then they will likely have a sturdy foundation to handle other problems. In fact, people have reported that race differences enabled them to explore other kinds of differences, thus broadening the perspectives of both parties. That education was invaluable because people who can fully appreciate the uniqueness of each individual are more likely to be better managers and leaders. Indeed, in my research on cross-race mentoring, mentors have frequently reported those relationships were the most fulfilling in terms of their own growth and transformation.

Network management

As discussed earlier, one of a mentor's key tasks is to help the protégé build a large and diverse network of relationships. The network must be strong enough to withstand even the loss of the mentor. Stephen Williams's mentor, for example, left the company after Williams had entered Stage 3 and was tackling increasingly challenging assignments.

From my research, I have found that the most effective network is heterogeneous along three dimensions. First, the network should have functional diversity; it should include mentors, sponsors, role models, peers, and even people whom the protégés themselves might be developing mentoring relationships toward. Second, the network should have variety with respect to position (seniors, colleagues, and juniors) as well as location (people within the immediate department, in other departments, and outside the organization). And third, the network should be demographically mixed in terms of race, gender, age, and culture.

Although a detailed description of the three dimensions is beyond the scope of this article, several points are worth noting. The difference between mentorship and sponsorship is that the former entails a much closer personal connection. Sponsors are coaches and advocates, whereas mentors are also counselors, friends, and in many ways surrogate family. Nevertheless, the role of sponsors can be critical when, for example, the protégé wants to pursue an opportunity outside the mentor's department. Also, especially when key decisions at an organization are made by committee, the protégé will benefit from having as many sponsors as possible.

A frequently overlooked area is a protégé's relationships with peers. People of color, in particular, can oftentimes become isolated from their peers due to resentment. But peer networks are crucial. For one thing, peers can help one another manage their careers and perform important self-assessments. They can be sympathetic sounding boards, useful information checks (what was your experience like when you first started in that division?), and helpful devil's advocates. For Stephen Williams, participation in a self-help group of African-Americans at his organization provided valuable social support and also expanded his network beyond his association with his engineering colleagues.

To ensure that a protégé is not missing any important peer relationships, the mentor must sometimes intervene. For example, if a mentor notices that his protégé is not part of an informal go-to-lunch crowd, he might assign her to a certain project with people in that group to encourage those friendships to form.

Another often overlooked area is a protégé's relationships with juniors, which will help the protégé become a valuable mentor in the future. Also, particularly for people in middle management, good relationships with junior staff can enable them to stay up-to-date with the latest technology. Furthermore, a protégé's mentors and superiors can be influenced greatly by the opinions of junior staff.

A network of relationships becomes vulnerable when it lacks any one of the dimensions. For example, if a person's network is limited to his organization, he will find it difficult to find employment else-where. On the other hand, people of color have the tendency to draw on a network from primarily outside their organizations. Such support can be invaluable, but it will provide little help when that individual is being considered for a highly desirable in house assign-ment. Establishing a diverse network is just the start—a person's network must be replenished and modified continually.

Creating the Environment for Success

Many mentors of minority professionals assume that their job begins and ends with the one-on-one relationships they establish with their protégés. This is hardly true. Mentors, especially those at the executive level, must do much more by actively supporting broader efforts and initiatives at their organizations to help create the conditions that foster the upward mobility of people of color. Specifically, they can do the following:

- Ensure that the pool of people being considered for promotions and key assignments reflects the diversity in the organization.

- Promote executive development workshops and seminars that address racial issues.

- Support in-house minority associations, including networking groups.

- Help colleagues manage their discomfort with race. In a meeting to decide whether someone of color should be promoted, for example, a person can help focus the discussion on the individual's actual performance while discounting racial issues disguised as legitimate concerns (such as vague criticisms that the managerial style of the minority candidate "doesn't fit in").

- Challenge implicit rules, such as those that assume that people who weren't fast movers early in their careers will never rise to the executive suites.

In conclusion, I should address one of the most insidious implicit rules of all: the two-tournament model. Many companies might be tempted to accept it as an empirical reality. Some might even want to make it policy by tacitly accepting that minorities cannot be fast-tracked in their early careers or by formally creating two separate career tournaments—one for whites and one for minorities. They assume that minorities will move more slowly in Stage 1. So, the thinking goes, why not take that time to ensure that high-potential minorities are overprepared to meet the social, technical, and racial challenges when they reach Stage 2?

I believe that any acceptance—let alone conscious replication—of the two-tournament system is a mistake. First, it unfairly institutionalizes the "tax" of added time that minorities have to pay as a result of existing racial barriers. As a consequence, a higher standard is set for their participation in the main competition for executive jobs. Second, such a policy would likely result in a number of high-performing and ambitious minorities leaving in Stage 1, before their careers could accelerate. It was beyond the scope of my study to determine exactly how many people of color with executive potential left during Stage 1, but I did encounter many executives who were surprised when their best minority talent left "just as good things were about to happen." Lastly, a two-tournament model could eventually lead to backlash among white plateaued managers who, not realizing that they had been passed over in Stage 1 because they were not deemed executive material, become resentful toward the promising minorities taking off in Stages 2 and 3.

But I am not advocating a one-tournament system of fast-tracking. After all, it is no accident that people of color haven't been fast-tracked in the past. One reason is that organizations have been largely ineffective in helping minorities establish relationships with mentors. Thus, artificially placing minority professionals onto a fast track without first changing the underlying process dynamics would set up those individuals for failure.

Organizations instead should provide a range of career paths, all uncorrelated with race, that lead to the executive suite. Ideally, this system of movement would allow variation across all groups—

people could move at their own speed through the three stages based on their individual strengths and needs, not their race. Achieving this system, however, would require integrating the principles of opportunity, development, and diversity into the fabric of the organization's management practices and human resource systems. And an important element in the process would be to identify potential mentors, train them, and ensure that they are paired with promising professionals of color.

Originally published in April 2001. Reprint R0104F

Leadership
in Your Midst

Tapping the Hidden Strengths of Minority Executives.
by Sylvia Ann Hewlett, Carolyn Buck Luce,
and Cornel West

ALL COMPANIES VALUE LEADERSHIP—some of them enough to invest
dearly in cultivating it. But few management teams seem to value
one engine of leadership development that is right under their noses,
churning out the kind of talent they need most. We're referring to the
deeply substantive outside lives of their minority executives.

If you know many minority professionals—particularly women
of color—then you know that these are the people who are called
upon inordinately to lend their energies, perspectives, and guidance
to activities outside their jobs. (We use the term "minority" in the
statistical sense to denote people who in terms of race or ethnicity are not in the majority in their corporations or organizations.)
Because they have "made it," and because often they have done so
against heavy odds, they are mentors of choice to young people in
their communities. Within their workplaces, they serve on numerous diversity-seeking task forces and spearhead minority recruitment efforts. They play high-profile volunteer roles in their towns,
schools, and churches, and the amount of time they invest in these
roles is substantial. In the words of Ella Bell, a professor at Dart-
mouth's Tuck School of Business, "They comprise the backbone of
religious organizations and provide a significant part of the energy
driving community service in the United States."

Off-the-job leadership development

Professional women of color incubate leadership and other transferable skills in their neighborhoods and communities. Specifically, the highly educated African-American women in our study develop cultural capital in the following ways:

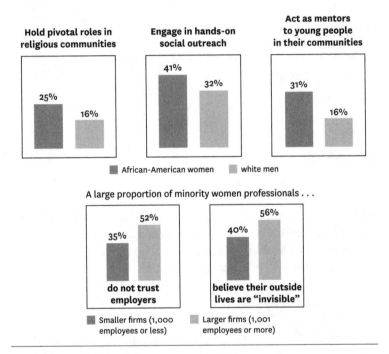

Hold pivotal roles in religious communities

25%
16%

Engage in hands-on social outreach

41%
32%

Act as mentors to young people in their communities

31%
16%

■ African-American women ■ white men

A large proportion of minority women professionals . . .

35%
52%
do not trust employers

40%
56%
believe their outside lives are "invisible"

■ Smaller firms (1,000 employees or less)   ■ Larger firms (1,001 employees or more)

For many minority professionals, involvement in such activities is an important, inherently satisfying part of their lives. For some, it's a way of giving back—or, more accurately, giving in turn the kind of help that benefited them early on. But it's also a fertile source of continued personal growth. In these myriad roles, minority professionals hone valuable leadership skills. The problem is that those skills are not properly recognized by their employers. And no conscious attempt is made to transfer them into the corporate environment and develop them further. The disproportionate load of care that minority professionals bear in their extended families is also

Idea in Brief

A company's leadership talent translates directly into competitive prowess. Yet many management teams are blind to one powerful engine of leadership development that's right under their noses: community work performed by minority professionals in their off-hours. Such work teaches professionals crucial leadership skills such as strategic planning, negotiation, financial savvy, and change management.

So why aren't more companies attuned to the treasure trove of leadership talent in their midst? Many minority professionals, fearful that their volunteer work in religious and ethnic organizations will earn them charges of being "different," hide the work from supervisors. Result? Their talents, passion, and dedication remain invisible—and untapped.

How to leverage the unseen strengths your minority professionals are honing outside the office? Develop an appreciation for community work. Use telecommuting and flexible schedules to ease the heavy burden minority leaders shoulder when they add community work to their family responsibilities. Combat hidden biases—such as disapproval of ethnic dress or mannerisms—that discourage minorities from revealing their nonwork lives. And help minority employees apply lessons learned from community work to your company's challenges.

As blockbuster companies such as General Electric, Unilever, and Time Warner have discovered, leveraging minority professionals' off-hours experience infuses your leadership talent pool with fresh energy, vital skills, and deep commitment to your company.

invisible to employers, and neither acknowledged nor supported by corporate benefits packages. The result: Too many high-potential employees end up feeling ignored and diminished, overextended and burned out. At the same time, organizations are being deprived of the strong and diverse leadership they could so easily draw upon.

In 2004, the Center for Work-Life Policy formed a private-sector task force called the Hidden Brain Drain to investigate the challenges faced by female and minority talent over the life span. In the spring of 2005, three member companies—Unilever, General Electric, and Time Warner—sponsored a cross-sectoral national survey and series of focus groups to discover the facts about minority professionals' outside leadership work and why it remains unrecognized.

Idea in Practice

To leverage your minority professionals' unseen strengths:

Appreciate Minority Community Work

Support minority community organizations with the same commitment that your company supports other community organizations such as the United Way.

> *Example:* Pitney Bowes supports Delta Sigma Theta sorority, a national African-American community service organization. It purchases advertising space in Delta Sigma Theta's fundraising journals and matches employees' donations. The company recruited one of its most talented black professionals through its participation in a leadership development program for minority youth sponsored by Delta Sigma Theta.

Lessen the Load

A disproportionate number of minority professionals shoulder responsibility not just for their immediate family, but for their extended families, too. Result? An extra-heavy workload that can lead to burnout.

To lessen their load, offer flextime and telecommuting. "Widen the tent" by offering employee benefits that address needs beyond nuclear family.

> *Example:* Time Warner changed its Employee Assistance Program policies to extend certain provisions to extended family members at no extra cost. It also extended back-up child-care programs and college planning to grandparents, uncles, and aunts. These relatively inexpensive benefits

(The exhibit "Off-the-job leadership development" describes the research.) A companion study, which targeted the global executives of a large multinational corporation, attests to the resonance of this research in other countries. (The sidebar "Invisible Lives in the Global Context" highlights some of these findings.)

The U.S. research, which we share here for the first time, underscores that the lives of minority professionals are rich with experience that goes unleveraged by their employers. But it also reveals a startling fact: These lives remain invisible largely by choice. For many reasons, minority professionals are reluctant to speak of their outside pursuits and accomplishments to colleagues and managers. We are left with a dual challenge: Companies can't leverage what they don't see—and they can't see what is purposely concealed.

have spurred a strong positive impact on minority recruitment and retention.

Embrace Diversity

"Walk the talk" in your diversity initiatives by evaluating managers on their track record in recruiting and retaining minority talent—and linking this evaluation to compensation.

Example: Lehman Brothers rewards senior managers who meet diversity goals with money from a bonus pool that's divided and awarded at the end of each year. The company's commitment to diversity attracts talented minorities—such as one black Wall Street banker who returned to the financial world after several years' hiatus and accepted an offer from Lehman Brothers because of its diversity policies.

Encourage "Action Learning"

Help minority professionals reflect on their off-hours community experiences, extract and generalize lessons, and apply their learning in your company.

Example: Goldman Sachs has encouraged one minority investment banker to serve as a board vice-president and fundraiser for the Lincoln Square Neighborhood Center, a nonprofit organization that supports low-income families who share a ZIP code with wealthy families. The role teaches her how to work with diverse individuals and motivate prospective donors to maximize their contributions—skills Goldman Sachs wants her to have.

Cultural Capital

One of the impressive professionals we encountered in our research is Sheryl Battles, an African-American vice president of corporate communications at a major global corporation. In addition to her primary responsibility managing executive and investor communications, she coordinates the corporation's communications on issues of diversity and in that capacity supports 30 to 40 events a year. It's a task that constitutes just 5% of her official job description but consumes roughly 25% of her 50-hour workweek. In her personal life, she speaks at community events and career seminars for minority students and is involved in the church that she, her husband, and their daughter attend. She is also on the board of a local organization for the arts and has been active in its African-American Cultural Heritage Series since its inception a decade ago.

Over the years, Sheryl has accumulated substantial cultural capital, sociologist Pierre Bourdieu's term for nonmonetary wealth and relationship capital generated outside the workplace. Cultural capital is impossible to measure with any precision but is undeniably vital for anyone who wishes to exert influence in a neighborhood, a company, or a nation. Everyone accumulates a measure of cultural capital in their lives, but in the case of minority professionals, it is unusually rich. Consider, for example, the value of Joyce's cultural capital. (All research participants referred to in this article by a first name only are disguised at their request.) Joyce is a change agent to be reckoned with in her community. In her church, she was recently inspired by a progressive pastor's vision for transforming the congregation's stance on a divisive social issue. At the same time, she knew he would face resistance—and that the intensity of his enthusiasm was blinding him to the harsh realities of making change happen. He needed a pragmatic strategist, and in her, he found one. Together they guided the church through the transition, crunching the numbers, outlining a plan, initiating a series of meetings with congregants, and evaluating progress. When we talked with Joyce, she reflected on the experience, noting the difficulty of simultaneously unleashing and controlling the energy that flows from transformational change.

Does all this sound like valuable leadership training? The irony is that, despite being a strategic planner at a *Fortune* 100 company, Joyce never heads up such comprehensive initiatives at work. "Sure, I develop strategic plans here," she reflects, "but my hands are tied half the time. [At church] I have an audience that says, 'Yeah, do your thing.'"

Beyond personal stories like these, statistics do even more to make the point. Among highly educated African-American female professionals, 25% are active leaders in their religious communities (compared with 16% of white men) and 41% are involved in social outreach activities (compared with 32% of white men). Most frequently, they volunteer in schools, hospitals, libraries, shelters, and other organizations in their communities. Minority women are also on the front lines helping young people in their communities as mentors, tutors, and "big sisters." A quarter of African-American businesswomen (25%) take on these roles. (The figure for white businesswomen is 14%).

Such substantive community involvement develops strategic and interpersonal skills, hones core values, and builds organizational and communication capabilities—all of which are transferable to and highly valued in the workplace. Yet our research shows that these skills remain invisible to managers.

Under the Radar

Why aren't companies more attuned to the untapped leadership in their ranks? First, because they haven't looked for it. Traditionally, to the extent that management takes an interest in employees' "extracurricular" lives, the focus has been on activities that have long been sanctioned by white male executives and are thought to burnish a company's image or enhance client relationships: United Way drives, symphony orchestra sponsorships, and sporting events, for example. Most companies do not bother to note the kind of pursuit that Stephanie, a bright, young African-American manager we interviewed, is involved in: running an award-winning Girl Scout troop in a homeless shelter. "These kids are not going to Harvard, they don't have a place to live, and they don't know how many times they're going to eat today," she told us. Stephanie's commitment to these homeless girls is expanding her leadership skill set as she navigates public- and nonprofit-sector bureaucracies while serving a population with myriad needs.

But Stephanie is convinced that her boss disapproves of her involvement in scouting, because it means she must leave work at 5:30 pm a few times a month. Despite the fact that she arrives at 7 am on those days, she is acutely concerned about being thought of as less than fully committed to her job. She refrains from talking

Invisible Lives in the Global Context

OUR RESEARCH SHOWS THAT MINORITY executives in the United States lead rich lives of leadership and responsibility that are largely invisible to their employers. Is the same true for global executives who do not share the dominant ethnicity of leaders at headquarters? To examine this question, we conducted an employee survey of one large company, a Europe-based multinational with extensive operations in the United Kingdom, India, and South Africa. Targeting midlevel managers and senior executives, we reached more than 1,900 employees. Our goal was to compare the experiences of a group of predominantly white executives in the UK (male and female) with those of a group of predominantly nonwhite executives in India and South Africa.

Like minority executives in the United States, this company's global executives are rich in cultural capital

- 30% of South African executives are leaders in their religious organizations (compared with 10% of executives in the UK)

- 20% of Indian executives serve as mentors to young people in their communities (the figure for UK executives is 8%)

- 38% of South African executives are involved in social outreach programs, as are 27% of Indian executives

Global executives deal with an inordinate load of care responsibilities

- 32% of Indian respondents have elders in their households, while in South Africa, 46% regularly care for elderly relatives outside their homes (only 3% of UK executives have elders living in their homes)

- 33% of Indian respondents support children from extended families and the community (for UK executives, the figure is 12%)

---

about her Girl Scouts program at work—even though this initiative earned her a Future Leader Today award at a ceremony at the White House.

Stephanie's reticence suggests a second reason that minority professionals' lives remain invisible to their managers: because they are deliberately hidden. Sometimes this is simply because professionals themselves don't recognize their outside affiliations as legitimate leadership development venues. One highly accomplished woman we met is on the board of an active and growing nonprofit organization, where she is gaining valuable skills in fundraising and

Many global executives suspect hidden bias and choose to keep information about their personal lives close to the vest

- 49% of South African executives perceive "style compliance" pressures

- 78% of respondents in India and South Africa believe that colleagues whose looks and style mirror senior management's are unfairly favored in promotions

- 48% of Indian executives don't fully trust their employer with information about their private lives (compared with 35% of UK executives)

- Almost half of nonwhite global executives say their outside lives are invisible to the company

Among the initiatives suggested by the survey to improve the situation, the following were favored by an overwhelming majority of global executives

- cultural sensitivity training to break down stereotypes (89% to 96%)

- better access to mentors (88% to 95%)

- safe harbors for discussing issues in their private lives while maintaining anonymity (77% to 86%)

- evaluation of individual managers' success in developing diverse talent based on input from subordinates (60% to 78%)

A detailed report of this survey's findings and its underlying methodology is available from the Center for Talent Innovation.

---

finance. But she told us, "I have not made the choice to share my board involvement at work. . . . I have never found a natural segue to make it relevant to what I do for the firm."

Sometimes the conversation doesn't occur because it would necessarily touch on religion, an important part of many minorities' nonwork lives. Joyce, the strategic planner we introduced earlier, feels she can't talk about the change effort she managed for her church, which is a different denomination from that of the apparently homogeneous hierarchy of leaders at her company. The same fear makes Michael, an Asian-American executive at a large California-based energy company, reluctant to share with colleagues his involvement on the board of a prominent charity. His reticence stems from the fact that the charity supports faith-based organizations and targets minority families. According to Michael, colleagues are likely to react negatively to his involvement because it raises "the big taboo subjects of the workplace: religion and ethnicity." In his view, it leads them to think, "You're *different*. I have always suspected that—and now you're confirming it." Michael admits that if people, himself included, talked more openly, then the taboos might be lifted, and his charity work might gain legitimacy and heft. But his short-term view is strictly pragmatic: "Why give anyone ammo?"

The fact that many minorities fear giving employers "ammunition" to use against them is among the most disturbing findings of our research. As shown in the chart below, many minority women professionals feel they cannot trust their employers with even basic information about their private lives. In large corporations, the percentage rises to more than half.

The survey data show that the distrust and reluctance to discuss private lives are deeply rooted in minorities' experiences of "hidden bias" in corporate cultures. Many avoid discussing their nonwork lives because they don't want to run the risk of reinforcing negative stereotypes. Latisha, an African-American executive at a global consumer products company, described growing up in the Newark projects, her mother on welfare and both parents eventually succumbing to AIDS. "When I do try and open up personally, people just don't get it . . . So you stop trying." Others worry about a perception that they got their jobs through affirmative action rather than on the grounds of merit.

Some feel hemmed in by "style compliance" issues, such as speaking style, hand gestures, and appearance. Nearly one-third of minority female executives (32%) in large corporations worry that their quiet speaking style is equated with lack of leadership potential, while 23% worry that their animated hand gestures are perceived as inappropriate. Fully 34% of African-American women in the business sector believe that promotion at their companies is based on appearance rather than ability.

According to Sears executive Angela Williams, hidden biases can be debilitating because they lead minority professionals to "deny their authenticity" in their efforts to fit into the prevailing white male model. Indeed, our research shows that almost one-fifth of professional women of color (19%) perceive hidden biases severe enough for them to consider quitting. Focus group participants talked about "teetering on the edge" (thinking about quitting, looking for a new job, trying to figure out whether there is less bias elsewhere) for months, or even years, meanwhile downsizing effort and expectations. One participant told us she had "quit but stayed on the job"—with predictable effects on performance.

Leveraging Unseen Strengths

Companies stand to benefit enormously if they can learn to nurture and support the cultural capital that minority professionals routinely develop outside work. Our research reveals four ways companies can discover and leverage these hidden skills: Companies need to build a greater awareness of the invisible lives of their minority professionals; they need to appreciate and try to lighten the outsize burdens these professionals carry; they must build trust in their ranks by putting teeth into diversity goals and encouraging more latitude in leadership style; and they should finish the job of leadership development begun in minorities' off-hours activities so that those nascent skills can make a difference to workplace performance and competitive strength.

Shine a light

First, greater awareness and appreciation of community work is key. A large number of minority women professionals (45%) do not feel that their roles and responsibilities outside the workplace are recognized or understood by their employers. Minority women in larger companies (56%), young women of color (50%), and Asian women (49%) are the most likely to feel that their lives are "invisible" to their employers.

Demitra Jones, on the other hand, has no such concern. A dedicated human resource generalist at Pitney Bowes, she feels her employer is fully supportive of the evenings and weekends she spends with her sorority sisters. When Demitra says "sorority," she's talking about Delta Sigma Theta, an African-American organization founded in 1913 that "places more emphasis on service than on socializing." Her membership in the organization is a strenuous commitment, demanding 30 hours a month on top of 60-hour workweeks. It's a win-win situation for her and for Pitney Bowes and has been since the beginning. It was a Delta Sigma Theta member who matched Demitra with the company even before she entered college through Inroads, a leadership development institute for minority youth. Since then, Pitney Bowes has continued to support Delta Sigma Theta in many ways, from purchasing advertising space in fundraising souvenir journals to matching Demitra's own donations. More important, it has kept an eye on the cultivation and training of Demitra as a leader in both worlds. It's no coincidence that her rapid rise in the company paralleled her progress through the leadership structure of the sorority, which she joined as a junior at Trinity College in Hartford, Connecticut.

What Pitney Bowes has done is not difficult; the company merely shined a light on an aspect of employee life that is often left in the shadows. This kind of light can take many forms. Some specific suggestions that came out of our survey include, for example, ensuring that recruiting activities are recognized explicitly in job descriptions and performance evaluations. Also, allowing employees to set aside time for volunteer activities—even a few hours a month—would send a message that employers recognize and value social outreach and community involvement. An overwhelming majority of our survey participants would welcome training from their companies in fundraising for volunteer activities. Companies could even take an active role in helping young minority professionals access nonprofit boards, thereby giving them an early opportunity to develop leadership skills they can bring back to their workplaces.

Lessen the load

Companies that are truly invested in seeing their diverse talent flourish must be better attuned to the extra burdens carried by many minorities—particularly minority women, whose load of care reaches beyond the nuclear family to extended family and the community. Over half of minority professional women are working mothers (51%), compared with 41% of professional white women. Many, too, are single moms or prime breadwinners. African-American professional women in our survey are more than twice as likely as white women to be single mothers (18%, compared with 7%). In addition, minority women spend significant amounts of time caring for elders and extended family. Seventeen percent of African-American female professionals care for elders and extended family, spending an average of 12.4 hours per week on this care. (The figures for professional white men and women are 6.6 and 9.5 hours, respectively.)

Given this heavy burden of care, some well-established practices like flextime and telecommuting may be especially attractive to minority professionals. Beyond these, there are forms of assistance that few companies have considered, but that might, at small expense, be of tremendous benefit. For example, in our survey there was considerable support for company initiatives that "widen the tent," such as employee benefits that go beyond the nuclear family. Nearly three-quarters (74%) of minority women want help paying for health insurance for up to two members of their extended families. Many minority women (72%) want a few days of annual leave for the purpose of elder care or extended-family care. And 74% of minority women say they would appreciate help in accessing state and federal services for a range of nuclear- and extended-family needs.

Time Warner is one company that has begun to address the issue. Patricia Fili-Krushel, executive vice president of administration, explains, "I wanted to check if we were looking through a white lens in terms of how we organize benefits—and, sure enough, we were." The company recently extended its employee assistance program (which includes, for example, access to child care referral services and company scholarship programs) to other reliant family members (perhaps an aunt or uncle). "In the last five months, there's been a 200% increase in uptake," she says. "There's a lot we can do that doesn't cost a lot of money. It just takes some different thinking."

Reimagine inclusion

The research data underscore the need to expand and amplify what is meant by inclusion. We're not talking here about the same old diversity initiatives, but specifically about innovative policies that build trust and foster workplace environments where minorities feel able to share the full round of their lives. Our survey revealed a widespread wish that companies establish "safe harbors"—places where employees can discuss issues, challenges, or opportunities in their private lives while maintaining anonymity. (Support for this notion was highest among Hispanic women professionals, at 75%, but it was also favored by majorities of African-American women, white women, and African-American men.)

Respondents in our survey also emphasize the need to "walk the talk" in diversity initiatives and put in place financial incentives to motivate managers. Fully 71% of minority businesswomen support the idea of evaluating managers on their track records in recruiting minority talent and favor linking this evaluation to compensation.

This was particularly important to Marie, a Wall Street professional coming back to the financial world after a few years doing client work. She wanted a company that not only had a diversity program, but had one with teeth. As an African-American woman, she was all too familiar with diversity initiatives that never seemed to amount to anything and diversity goals that were never evaluated past their inception. When Marie started work at Lehman Brothers, she was encouraged by the firm's sizable diversity bonus pool—an incentive that recognizes individual managers and teams for their innovative diversity initiatives. The fact that her new firm encouraged investment bankers to take diversity seriously by providing meaningful incentives was a source of reassurance for Marie.

At Time Warner, there is a policy that for any hire at the vice president level or above, the slate of candidates must be diverse. In 2002, the company created the role of executive connector to make sure that there are viable candidates available for consideration. The connector uses contacts in numerous social and professional circles to develop an extensive pool of diverse candidates. Since taking on this role, Debra Langford has been instrumental in the hiring of 65 minority senior executives. She travels frequently to events and conferences looking for talented high-potential candidates. Once Debra has facilitated a minority hire, she monitors his or her progress. She knows that, unlike their white counterparts, the individuals may not have preexisting relationships within the company. Debra organizes formal and informal gatherings of employees with similar backgrounds—for instance, a lunch for African-American fathers or a dinner for minority lawyers.

Minority professionals are also reassured when they see companies actively combating hidden bias. According to DeAnne Aguirre, a senior vice president at Booz Allen Hamilton, a good way to begin is to "examine the prevailing mode of managerial behavior, determine where it is narrowly drawn, and reenvisage a much more inclusive model." In our survey, 72% of minority women back cultural sensitivity training for managers to break down stereotypes.

One company that has historically welcomed diversity and champions the notion of bringing one's whole self to work is Unilever. Through its Getting into the Skin program, introduced in 2002 as a key part of the company's leadership development program, Unilever takes direct aim at hidden biases by asking selected groups of current and future leaders to spend time outside the realm of their normal experiences. Former Unilever co-chairman Niall FitzGerald helped create the program and was also a participant. Of a 2002 journey to Croatia, he remarked, "I lived the life of a Salvation Army volunteer and picked up an unkempt, uncared-for man off the street . . . we talked about his life. In an eerie twist of fate, he turned out to be from my hometown. We were two people who fate had dealt very different hands. He taught me, in a way no other experience has, the power of generous listening— without judgment." Other participants have spent time at a rural hospital in Mexico, an AIDS clinic in Ireland, and a prison in Germany. The current CEO Patrick Cescau continues to build on Unilever's mission of inclusion and has established a diversity board, which he chairs.

Finish the job of leadership development

Companies will reap the most benefit from the outside leadership experiences of their employees when they begin to consider this cultural capital explicitly as a form of leadership "action learning." What this means is that they should observe established pedagogical practice, helping minority executives reflect on their experiences, extract and generalize the lessons, and apply what's been learned to other settings.

Some leading corporations are beginning to view after-hours work as leadership training. Goldman Sachs is one, says Aynesh Johnson, an investment banker at Goldman. With the firm's full knowledge and encouragement, Aynesh is sharpening her people skills by working as a board vice president for the Lincoln Square Neighborhood Center, a nonprofit organization that supports public housing residents who happen to share a zip code with some of the richest people in the world. In the process of figuring out how to fund-raise for these families, Aynesh has taken on a marketing task so challenging it would serve admirably as a business school case study. "It's a very rich and wonderful opportunity," Aynesh says, carefully. "But it's not glamorous." Nevertheless, Aynesh is proud to call her position on the center's board "part of my career." Describing her volunteer work, Aynesh says "it has taught me how to work with a wide range of individuals . . . maximizing their contributions." She's also learned how to listen gracefully when a prospective donor says no and how to refuse (also gracefully) to take no for an answer. These are skills her superiors at Goldman Sachs think are important. As a result, at work she does not hesitate to be open about this outside commitment. "Managers know, all the way up to the executive suite."

Another way to transfer cultural capital to the workplace is through networks of mentors. Many minority businesswomen are skilled mentors themselves, having reached out to young people in their own communities. They therefore know the potential of these relationships and feel frustrated when they lack mentors in their own organizations. In our survey, a significant proportion of minority professionals (66%) supported the creation of mentoring programs across divisions and the matching of minority employees with senior colleagues from similar ethnic and cultural backgrounds.

About the Research

STATISTICS IN THIS ARTICLE ARE the findings of a 2005 survey, fielded by Charney Research under the auspices of the Center for Work-Life Policy. The targeted survey sample comprised 1,601 professionals in the United States, ages 28 to 55, with college or professional degrees. This included 1,001 minority women (of whom one-third were African-American, one-third were Hispanic, and one-third were Asian), 200 minority men (also equally divided among the three groups), 198 white women, and 202 white men. The survey targeted people equally in four professional areas: medicine, law, education, and business and accounting. Interviews averaged 20 minutes and were conducted by telephone between January 2005 and February 2005. (A detailed report of the findings is available at www.talentinnovation.org.)

When mentors build trusting, open relationships with minority protégés, companies gain an important window on leadership talent that is often hidden from view. Mentors can actively engage their protégés in discussions about their outside roles and work with them to apply and enhance those skills in their everyday jobs.

General Electric provides much-needed access to mentors and actively fosters leadership along the way through affinity networks. The African-American Forum is a case in point. It began informally— 15 black managers coming together to study retention problems— and has grown into a major initiative that both serves as a vehicle through which minority employees find mentors and holds an annual meeting that draws nearly 1,400 people and features top executives. GE has integrated the AAF into succession planning. As Deborah Elam, manager of diversity and inclusive leadership, explains, "The practice of taking high-potential employees and placing them in leadership roles within the AAF allows top executives to better see the strengths of talented minority professionals."

Lives Made Visible

In 1952, Ralph Waldo Ellison published his classic novel, *Invisible Man*. His central insight remains relevant more than 50 years later: Those rendered "invisible" may well be the key to maintaining America's prosperity and integrity. This past half century has seen a sea change in terms of the opportunities available to minorities—especially female minorities. In response to the antidiscrimination laws of the 1960s and 1970s and the global talent shifts of the past 15 years, the face of power has begun to change. One only need look around the workplace. Whether you're talking Wall Street, Main Street, or the White House, most management teams now include powerful and conspicuous nonwhite talent. Secretary of State Condoleezza Rice, Avon CEO Andrea Jung, and Time Warner CEO Dick Parsons are cases in point.

Still, the belief among many minority professionals that they must somehow cloak their real identities has been extremely debilitating. Every professional, no matter what color or creed, wants to be recognized, appreciated, and supported. As we can see from these new data, for a substantial number of minority professionals, covering up outside lives and staying below the radar has produced isolation, alienation, distrust, and disengagement, all of which helps explain why progress has stalled. According to Catalyst and other research organizations, the data show that minorities are not being promoted or advanced at a rate commensurate with their representation in the talent pool. They remain bunched in the early stretches of the career highway. Few make it into the fast lane.

Any company that hopes to compete on the world stage using superior leadership talent must look squarely at the problem of hidden lives and resolve to overcome it. The key is to value the cultural capital that minorities routinely develop in their communities and bring this to bear in their workplaces. Think of the extraordinary energy and purpose that will be released when minority professionals are finally able to speak openly and proudly of their lives, their core values, and their skills. It might well be transformative—of individuals, of companies, and of society.

Originally published in November 2005. Reprint R0511D

What Most People Get Wrong About Men and Women

by Catherine H. Tinsley and Robin J. Ely

THE CONVERSATION ABOUT THE TREATMENT of women in the workplace has reached a crescendo of late, and senior leaders—men as well as women—are increasingly vocal about a commitment to gender parity. That's all well and good, but there's an important catch. The discussions, and many of the initiatives companies have undertaken, too often reflect a faulty belief: that men and women are fundamentally *different,* by virtue of their genes or their upbringing or both. Of course, there are biological differences. But those are not the differences people are usually talking about. Instead, the rhetoric focuses on the idea that women are inherently unlike men in terms of disposition, attitudes, and behaviors. (Think headlines that tout "Why women do X at the office" or "Working women don't Y.")

One set of assumed differences is marshaled to explain women's failure to achieve parity with men: Women negotiate poorly, lack confidence, are too risk-averse, or don't put in the requisite hours at work because they value family more than their careers. Simultaneously, other assumed differences—that women are more caring, cooperative, or mission-driven—are used as a rationale for companies to invest in women's success. But whether framed as a barrier or a benefit, these beliefs hold women back. We will not level the playing field so long as the bedrock on which it rests is our conviction about how the sexes are different.

The reason is simple: Science, by and large, does not actually support these claims. There is wide variation among women and among men, and meta-analyses show that, on average, the sexes are far more similar in their inclinations, attitudes, and skills than popular opinion would have us believe. We do see sex differences in various settings, including the workplace—but those differences are not rooted in fixed gender traits. Rather, they stem from organizational structures, company practices, and patterns of interaction that position men and women differently, creating systematically different experiences for them. When facing dissimilar circumstances, people respond differently—not because of their sex but because of their situations.

Emphasizing sex differences runs the risk of making them seem natural and inevitable. As anecdotes that align with stereotypes are told and retold, without addressing why and when stereotypical behaviors appear, sex differences are exaggerated and take on a determinative quality. Well-meaning but largely ineffectual interventions then focus on "fixing" women or accommodating them rather than on changing the circumstances that gave rise to different behaviors in the first place.

Take, for example, the common belief that women are more committed to family than men are. Research simply does not support that notion. In a study of Harvard Business School graduates that one of us conducted, nearly everyone, regardless of gender, placed a higher value on their families than on their work (see "Rethink What You 'Know' About High-Achieving Women," HBR, December 2014). Moreover, having made career decisions to accommodate family responsibilities didn't explain the gender achievement gap. Other research, too, makes it clear that men and women do not have fundamentally different priorities.

Numerous studies show that what does differ is the treatment mothers and fathers receive when they start a family. Women (but not men) are seen as needing support, whereas men are more likely to get the message—either explicit or subtle—that they need to "man up" and not voice stress and fatigue. If men do ask, say, for a lighter travel schedule, their supervisors may cut them some

Idea in Brief

The Belief

There's a popular notion that men and women are fundamentally different in important (nonbiological) ways—and those differences are cited to explain women's lagged achievement.

The Truth

According to numerous meta-analyses of published research, men and women are actually very similar with respect to key attributes such as confidence, appetite for risk, and negotiating skill.

Why It Matters

Too many managers try to "fix" women or accommodate their supposed differences—and that doesn't work. Companies must instead address the organizational conditions that lead to lower rates of retention and promotion for women.

---

slack—but often grudgingly and with the clear expectation that the reprieve is temporary. Accordingly, some men attempt an under-the-radar approach, quietly reducing hours or travel and hoping it goes unnoticed, while others simply concede, limiting the time they spend on family responsibilities and doubling down at work. Either way, they maintain a reputation that keeps them on an upward trajectory. Meanwhile, mothers are often expected, indeed encouraged, to ratchet back at work. They are rerouted into less taxing roles and given less "demanding" (read: lower-status, less career-enhancing) clients.

To sum up, men's and women's desires and challenges about work/family balance are remarkably similar. It is what they experience at work once they become parents that puts them in very different places.

Things don't have to be this way. When companies observe differences in the overall success rates of women and men, or in behaviors that are critical to effectiveness, they can actively seek to understand the organizational conditions that might be responsible, and then they can experiment with changing those conditions.

Consider the example of a savvy managing director concerned about the leaky pipeline at her professional services firm. Skeptical that women were simply "opting out" following the birth of a child, she investigated and found that one reason women were leaving the firm stemmed from the performance appraisal system: Supervisors had to adhere to a forced distribution when rating their direct reports, and women who had taken parental leave were unlikely to receive the highest rating because their performance was ranked against that of peers who had worked a full year. Getting less than top marks not only hurt their chances of promotion but also sent a demoralizing message that being a mother was incompatible with being on a partner track. However, the fix was relatively easy: The company decided to reserve the forced distribution for employees who worked the full year, while those with long leaves could roll over their rating from the prior year. That applied to both men and women, but the policy was most heavily used by new mothers. The change gave women more incentive to return from maternity leave and helped keep them on track for advancement. Having more mothers stay on track, in turn, helped chip away at assumptions within the firm about women's work/family preferences.

As this example reveals, companies need to dive deeper into their beliefs, norms, practices, and policies to understand how they position women relative to men and how the different positions fuel inequality. Seriously investigating the context that gives rise to differential patterns in the way men and women experience the workplace—and intervening accordingly—can help companies chart a path to gender parity.

Below, we address three popular myths about how the sexes differ and explain how each manifests itself in organizational discourse about women's lagged advancement. Drawing on years of social science research, we debunk the myths and offer alternative explanations for observed sex differences—explanations that point to ways that managers can level the playing field. We then offer a four-pronged strategy for undertaking such actions.

Popular Myths

We've all heard statements in the media and in companies that women lack *the desire or ability to negotiate,* that they lack *confidence,* and that they lack *an appetite for risk.* And, the thinking goes, those shortcomings explain why women have so far failed to reach parity with men.

For decades, studies have examined sex differences on these three dimensions, enabling social scientists to conduct meta-analyses— investigations that reveal whether or not, on average across studies, sex differences hold, and if so, how large the differences are. (See the sidebar "The Power of Meta-Analysis.") Just as importantly, meta-analyses also reveal the circumstances under which differences between men and women are more or less likely to arise. The aggregated findings are clear: Context explains any sex differences that exist in the workplace.

Take negotiation. Over and over, we hear that women are poor negotiators—they "settle too easily," are "too nice," or are "too cooperative." But not so, according to research. Jens Mazei and colleagues recently analyzed more than 100 studies examining whether men and women negotiate different outcomes; they determined that gender differences were small to negligible. Men have a slight advantage in negotiations when they are advocating exclusively for themselves and when ambiguity about the stakes or opportunities is high. Larger disparities in outcomes occur when negotiators either have no prior experience or are forced to negotiate, as in a mandated training exercise. But such situations are atypical, and even when they do arise, statisticians would deem the resulting sex differences to be small. As for the notion that women are more cooperative than men, research by Daniel Balliet and colleagues refutes that.

The belief that women lack confidence is another fallacy. That assertion is commonly invoked to explain why women speak up less in meetings and do not put themselves forward for promotions unless they are 100% certain they meet all the job requirements. But research does not corroborate the idea that women are less confident than men. Analyzing more than 200 studies, Kristen Kling and colleagues concluded that the only noticeable differences occurred during adolescence; starting at age 23, differences become negligible.

What about risk taking—are women really more conservative than men? Many people believe that's true—though they are split on whether being risk-averse is a strength or a weakness. On the

The Power of Meta-Analysis

A META-ANALYSIS IS A statistical technique used to combine the results of many studies, providing a more reliable basis for drawing conclusions from research. This approach has three advantages over a single study.

First, it is more *accurate*, because it is based on a very large sample—the total of the samples across all the studies—and because it contains data collected in many different contexts. Any single set of findings may reflect idiosyncrasies of the study's sample or context and thus may not yield conclusions that are truly generalizable. A meta-analysis, in essence, averages across these idiosyncrasies to give us a truer answer to the research question (in this case, "Are men and women different with regard to a particular trait or behavior?").

Second, a meta-analysis is more *comprehensive*. Because it contains studies conducted in many different contexts, it can tell us in which kinds of contexts we are more or less likely to see sex differences.

Third, a meta-analysis is more *precise:* It can tell us just how different men and women are. For any given trait or behavior, there is variability *among* men and *among* women; typically, those within-group differences are distributed around some "true" average for each group. Using the averages and the variability within each group, we can calculate an "effect size" that can be thought of as the impact that sex has on a particular trait. When testing for a sex difference, we are in essence asking the question "How much overlap is there between women and men, or, stated another way, how far apart are their respective averages, relative to the variability within each sex?"

Take the graph on the left below, which shows the distribution of men's and women's heights in the UK. We can see from the curves that men, on average, are quite a bit taller than women. In fact, men average five feet, nine inches, and women five feet, three inches—a six-inch difference. We can also see

positive side, the thinking goes, women are less likely to get caught up in macho displays of bluff and bravado and thus are less likely to take unnecessary risks. Consider the oft-heard sentiment following the demise of Lehman Brothers: "If Lehman Brothers had been Lehman Sisters, the financial crisis might have been averted." On the negative side, women are judged as too cautious to make high-risk, potentially high-payoff investments.

But once again, research fails to support either of these stereotypes. As with negotiation, sex differences in the propensity to that a number of women are taller than the average man, just as a number of men are shorter than the average woman. The size of the sex effect on height is 1.72, which is considered "large."

Using that sex difference as a reference point, we can see from the graph on the right that the difference between men and women in self-esteem, or confidence, is much smaller, with an effect size of 0.10. Although the difference in each graph is statistically significant, the difference in confidence is considered, from a statistical point of view, "trivial"—and from a managerial point of view, essentially meaningless. This same analysis for men's and women's negotiation outcomes and for their propensity to take risks yielded effect sizes of 0.20 ("small") and 0.13 ("trivial"), respectively. In short, contrary to popular belief, all three sex differences we consider in this article are, for all intents and purposes, meaningless.

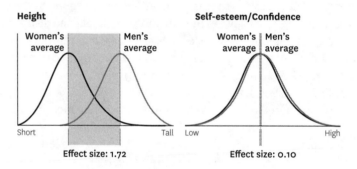

Note: Statisticians consider an effect size of less than 0.20 to be "trivial," 0.20–0.49 to be "small," 0.50–0.79 to be "medium," and 0.80 or more to be "large."

take risks are small and depend on the context. In a meta-analysis performed by James Byrnes and colleagues, the largest differences arise in contexts unlikely to exist in most organizations (such as among people asked to participate in a game of pure chance). Similarly, in a study Peggy Dwyer and colleagues ran examining the largest, last, and riskiest investments made by nearly 2,000 mutual fund investors, sex differences were very small. More importantly, when investors' specific knowledge about the investments was added to the equation, the sex difference diminished to near extinction, suggesting that access to information, not propensity for risk taking, explains the small sex differences that have been documented.

In short, a wealth of evidence contradicts each of these popular myths. Yet they live on through oft-repeated narratives routinely invoked to explain women's lagged advancement.

More-Plausible Explanations

The extent to which employees are able to thrive and succeed at work depends partly on the kinds of opportunities and treatment they receive. People are more likely to behave in ways that undermine their chances for success when they are disconnected from information networks, when they are judged or penalized disproportionately harshly for mistakes or failures, and when they lack feedback. Unfortunately, women are more likely than men to encounter each of these situations. And the way they respond—whether that's by failing to drive a hard bargain, to speak up, or to take risks—gets unfairly attributed to "the way women are," when in fact the culprit is very likely the differential conditions they face.

Multiple studies show, for example, that women are less embedded in networks that offer opportunities to gather vital information and garner support. When people lack access to useful contacts and information, they face a disadvantage in negotiations. They may not know what is on the table, what is within the realm of possibility, or even that a chance to strike a deal exists. When operating under such conditions, women are more likely to conform to the gender stereotype that "women don't ask."

We saw this dynamic vividly play out when comparing the experiences of two professionals we'll call Mary and Rick. (In this example and others that follow, we have changed the names and some details to maintain confidentiality.) Mary and Rick were both midlevel advisers in the wealth management division of a financial services firm. Rick was able to bring in more assets to manage because he sat on the board of a nonprofit, giving him access to a pool of potential clients with high net worth. What Mary did not know for many years is how Rick had gained that advantage. Through casual conversations with one of the firm's senior partners, with whom he regularly played tennis, Rick had learned that discretionary funds existed to help advisers cultivate relationships with clients. So he arranged for the firm to make a donation to the nonprofit. He then began attending the nonprofit's fund-raising events and hobnobbing with key players, eventually parlaying his connections into a seat on the board. Mary, by contrast, had no informal relationships with senior partners at the firm and no knowledge of the level of resources that could have helped her land clients.

When people are less embedded, they are also less aware of opportunities for stretch assignments and promotions, and their supervisors may be in the dark about their ambitions. But when women fail to "lean in" and seek growth opportunities, it is easy to assume that they lack the confidence to do so—not that they lack pertinent information. Julie's experience is illustrative. Currently the CEO of a major investment fund, Julie had left her previous employer of 15 years after learning that a more junior male colleague had leapfrogged over her to fill an opening she didn't even know existed. When she announced that she was leaving and why, her boss was surprised. He told her that if he had realized she wanted to move up, he would have gladly helped position her for the promotion. But because she hadn't put her hat in the ring, he had assumed she lacked confidence in her ability to handle the job.

How people react to someone's mistake or failure can also affect that person's ability to thrive and succeed. Several studies have found that because women operate under a higher-resolution microscope than their male counterparts do, their mistakes and failures are scrutinized more carefully and punished more severely. People who are scrutinized more carefully will, in turn, be less likely to speak up in meetings, particularly if they feel no one has their back. However, when women fail to speak up, it is commonly assumed that they lack confidence in their ideas.

We saw a classic example of this dynamic at a biotech company in which team leaders noticed that their female colleagues, all highly qualified research scientists, participated far less in team meetings than their male counterparts did, yet later, in one-on-one conversations, often offered insightful ideas germane to the discussion. What these leaders had failed to see was that when women did speak in meetings, their ideas tended to be either ignored until a man restated them or shot down quickly if they contained even the slightest flaw. In contrast, when men's ideas were flawed, the meritorious elements were salvaged. Women therefore felt they needed to be 110% sure of their ideas before they would venture to share them. In a context in which being smart was the coin of the realm, it seemed better to remain silent than to have one's ideas repeatedly dismissed.

It stands to reason that people whose missteps are more likely to be held against them will also be less likely to take risks. That was the case at a Big Four accounting firm that asked us to investigate why so few women partners were in formal leadership roles. The reason, many believed, was that women did not want such roles because of their family responsibilities, but our survey revealed a more complex story. First, women and men were equally likely to say they would accept a leadership role if offered one, but men were nearly 50% more likely to have been offered one. Second, women were more likely than men to say that worries about jeopardizing their careers deterred them from pursuing leadership positions— they feared they would not recover from failure and thus could not afford to take the risks an effective leader would need to take. Research confirms that such concerns are valid. For example, studies by Victoria Brescoll and colleagues found that if women in male-dominated occupations make mistakes, they are accorded less status and seen as less competent than men making the same mistakes; a study by Ashleigh Rosette and Robert Livingston demonstrated that black women leaders are especially vulnerable to this bias.

Research also shows that women get less frequent and lower-quality feedback than men. When people don't receive feedback, they are less likely to know their worth in negotiations. Moreover, people who receive little feedback are ill-equipped to assess their strengths, shore up their weaknesses, and judge their prospects for success and are therefore less able to build the confidence they need to proactively seek promotions or make risky decisions.

Why the Sex-Difference Narrative Persists

BELIEFS IN SEX DIFFERENCES HAVE staying power partly because they uphold conventional gender norms, preserve the gender status quo, and require no upheaval of existing organizational practices or work arrangements. But they are also the path of least resistance for our brains. Three well-documented cognitive errors help explain the endurance of the sex-difference narrative.

First, when seeking to explain others' behavior, we gravitate to explanations based on intrinsic *personality traits*—including stereotypically "male" traits and stereotypically "female" traits"—rather than *contextual factors*. (Social psychologists call this "the fundamental attribution error.") For example, if a man speaks often and forcefully in a meeting, we are more likely to conclude that he is assertive and confident than to search for a situational explanation, such as that he's been repeatedly praised for his contributions. Likewise, if a woman is quiet in a meeting, the easier explanation is that she's meek or underconfident; it takes more cognitive energy to construct an alternative account, such as that she is used to being cut off or ignored when she speaks. In short, when we see men and women behaving in gender-stereotypical ways, we tend to make the most cognitively simple assumption—that the behavior reflects who they are rather than the situation they are in.

Second, mere exposure to a continuing refrain, such as "Women are X, and men are Y," makes people judge the statement as true. Many beliefs—that bats are blind, that fresh produce is always more nutritious than frozen, that you shouldn't wake a sleepwalker—are repeated so often that their mere familiarity makes them easier for our minds to accept as truth. (This is called the "mere exposure effect.")

Third, once people believe something is true, they tend to seek, notice, and remember evidence that confirms the position and to ignore or forget evidence that would challenge it. (Psychologists call this "confirmation bias.") If we believe that gender stereotypes are accurate, we are more likely to expect, notice, and remember times when men and women behave in gender-stereotypical ways and to overlook times when they don't.

An example of this dynamic comes from a consulting firm in which HR staff members delivered partners' annual feedback to associates. The HR folks noticed that when women were told they were "doing fine," they "freaked out," feeling damned by faint praise; when men received the same feedback, they left the meeting "feeling great." HR concluded that women lack self-confidence and

are therefore more sensitive to feedback, so the team advised partners to be especially encouraging to the women associates and to
soften any criticism. Many of the partners were none too pleased
to have to treat a subset of their associates with kid gloves, grous-
ing that "if women can't stand the heat, they should get out of the
kitchen." What these partners failed to realize, however, is that the
kitchen was a lot hotter for women in the firm than for men. Why?
Because the partners felt more comfortable with the men and so
were systematically giving them more informal, day-to-day feedback. When women heard in their annual review that they were
doing "fine," it was often the first feedback they'd received all year;
they had nothing else to go on and assumed it meant their performance was merely adequate. In contrast, when men heard they were
doing "fine," it was but one piece of information amidst a steady
stream. The upshot was disproportionate turnover among women
associates, many of whom left the firm because they believed their
prospects for promotion were slim.

An Alternative Approach

The problem with the sex-difference narrative is that it leads companies to put resources into "fixing" women, which means that women
miss out on what they need—and what every employee deserves: a
context that enables them to reach their potential and maximizes
their chances to succeed.

Managers who are advancing gender equity in their firms are taking a more inquisitive approach—rejecting old scripts, seeking an
evidence-based understanding of how women experience the workplace, and then creating the conditions that increase women's prospects for success. Their approach entails four steps:

1. Question the narrative

A consulting firm we worked with had recruited significant numbers of talented women into its entry ranks—and then struggled
to promote them. Their supervisors' explanations? Women are
insufficiently competitive, lack "fire in the belly," or don't have the

requisite confidence to excel in the job. But those narratives did not ring true to Sarah, a regional head, because a handful of women—those within her region—were performing and advancing at par. So rather than accept her colleagues' explanations, she got curious.

2. Generate a plausible alternative explanation

Sarah investigated the factors that might have helped women in her region succeed and found that they received more hands-on training and more attention from supervisors than did women in other regions. This finding suggested that the problem lay not with women's deficiencies but with their differential access to the conditions that enhance self-confidence and success.

To test that hypothesis, Sarah designed an experiment, with our help. First, we randomly split 60 supervisors into two groups of 30 for a training session on coaching junior consultants. Trainers gave both groups the same lecture on how to be a good coach. With one group, however, trainers shared research showing that differences in men's and women's self-confidence are minuscule, thus subtly giving the members of this "treatment" group reason to question gender stereotypes. The "control" group didn't get that information. Next, trainers gave all participants a series of hypotheticals in which an employee—sometimes a man and sometimes a woman—was underperforming. In both groups, participants were asked to write down the feedback they would give the underperforming employee.

Clear differences emerged between the two groups. Supervisors in the control group took different tacks with the underperforming man and woman: They were far less critical of the woman and focused largely on making her feel good, whereas they gave the man feedback that was more direct, specific, and critical, often with concrete suggestions for how he could improve. In contrast, the supervisors who had been shown research that refuted sex differences in self-confidence gave both employees the same kind of feedback; they also asked for more-granular information about the employee's performance so that they could deliver constructive comments. We were struck by how the participants who had been given a reason to question gender stereotypes focused on learning more about individuals' specific performance problems.

The experiment confirmed Sarah's sense that women's lagged advancement might be due at least partly to supervisors' assumptions about the training and development needs of their female direct reports. Moreover, her findings gave supervisors a plausible alternative explanation for women's lagged advancement—a necessary precondition for taking the next step. Although different firms find different types of evidence more or less compelling—not all require as rigorous a test as this firm did—Sarah's evidence-based approach illustrates a key part of the strategy we are advocating.

3. Change the context and assess the results

Once a plausible alternative explanation has been developed, companies can make appropriate changes and see if performance improves. Two stories help illustrate this step. Both come from a midmarket private equity firm that was trying to address a problem that had persisted for 10 years: The company's promotion and retention rates for white women and people of color were far lower than its hiring rates.

The first story involves Elaine, an Asian-American senior associate who wanted to sharpen her financing skills and asked Dave, a partner, if she could assist with that aspect of his next deal. He invited her to lunch, but when they met, he was underwhelmed. Elaine struck him as insufficiently assertive and overly cautious. He decided against putting her on his team—but then he had second thoughts. The partners had been questioning their ability to spot and develop talent, especially in the case of associates who didn't look like them. Dave thus decided to try an experiment: He invited Elaine to join the team and then made a conscious effort to treat her exactly as he would have treated someone he deemed a superstar. He introduced her to the relevant players in the industry, told the banks she would be leading the financing, and gave her lots of rope but also enough feedback and coaching so that she wouldn't hang herself. Elaine did not disappoint; indeed, her performance was stellar. While quiet in demeanor, Dave's new protégée showed an uncanny ability to read the client and come up with creative approaches to the deal's financing.

A second example involves Ned, a partner who was frustrated that Joan, a recent-MBA hire on his team, didn't assert herself on management team calls. At first Ned simply assumed that Joan lacked confidence. But then it occurred to him that he might be falling back on gender stereotypes, and he took a closer look at his own behavior. He realized that he wasn't doing anything to make participation easier for her and was actually doing things that made it harder, like taking up all the airtime on calls. So they talked about it, and Joan admitted that she was afraid of making a mistake and was hyperaware that if she spoke, she needed to say something very smart. Ned realized that he, too, was afraid she would make a mistake or wouldn't add value to the discussion, which is partly why he took over. But on reflection, he saw that it wouldn't be the end of the world if she did stumble—he did the same himself now and again. For their next few calls, they went over the agenda beforehand and worked out which parts she would take the lead on; he then gave her feedback after the call. Ned now has a junior colleague to whom he can delegate more; Joan, meanwhile, feels more confident and has learned that she can take risks and recover from mistakes.

4. Promote continual learning

Both Dave and Ned recognized that their tendency to jump to conclusions based on stereotypes was robbing them—and the firm—of vital talent. Moreover, they have seen firsthand how questioning assumptions and proactively changing conditions gives women the opportunity to develop and shine. The lessons from these small-scale experiments are ongoing: Partners at the firm now meet regularly to discuss what they're learning. They also hold one another accountable for questioning and testing gender-stereotypical assessments as they arise. As a result, old narratives about women's limitations are beginning to give way to new narratives about how the firm can better support all employees.

The four steps we've outlined are consistent with research suggesting that on difficult issues such as gender and race, managers respond more positively when they see themselves as part of the solution rather than simply part of the problem. The solution to women's lagged advancement is not to fix women or their managers but to fix the conditions that undermine women and reinforce gender stereotypes. Furthermore, by taking an inquisitive, evidence-based approach to understanding behavior, companies can not only address gender disparities but also cultivate a learning orientation and a culture that gives all employees the opportunity to reach their full potential.

Originally published in May–June 2018. Reprint R1803J

Hacking Tech's Diversity Problem

by Joan C. Williams

WHEN GOOGLE, YAHOO, LINKEDIN, AND Facebook disclosed their woefully low levels of female employment in the summer of 2014, admitting that they had a lot of work to do to improve them, they signaled a shift for the technology industry. It's remarkable that the sector is finally stepping up to the plate on diversity—and refreshing that its focus is on metrics rather than rhetoric.

Make no mistake: Improving those metrics will be challenging. A key feature of the tech culture—the shared belief that it's a meritocracy—may work against change. An important study by Emilio J. Castilla and Stephen Benard has shown that when an organization's core values state that raises and promotions are "based entirely on the performance of the employee"—in other words, when a company sees itself as a meritocracy—women are actually more likely to get smaller bonuses than men with equivalent performance reviews. Subtle biases against women are clearly at work here. Moreover, 40 years of social science have taught us that such biases will be perpetuated unless they're *intentionally* interrupted, and people who think they work for meritocracies are less likely to do what it takes to interrupt them.

On the other hand, if tech's senior leaders are serious about gender diversity, they could be perfectly positioned to lead change. As they so often remind us, they're not about business as usual. They're out to change the world, with corporate mottoes like "Don't be evil" and "Move fast and break things." One thing I hope they'll break with is the "diversity industrial complex": the standard approach of making token hires, offering sensitivity training, setting up mentoring networks, and introducing other incremental changes that focus on altering women's behavior to, say, make them better negotiators. When an organization lacks diversity, it's not the employees who need fixing. It's the business systems.

This article is intended to help tech companies—and others— fix those systems. It describes a new metrics-based approach that pulls from the lean start-up playbook: Collect detailed data about whether gender bias plays a role in daily workplace interactions; identify company-specific ways to measure its effect; create hypotheses about what "interrupters" might move those metrics; and then throw some spaghetti at the wall and see what sticks. Measure what happened, adjust your hypotheses, and do it all over again until you get it right.

What's a Bias Interrupter?

While much of the social science research is still devoted to "admiring the problem"—demonstrating the same patterns of gender bias over and over—some studies have begun to explore how to interrupt bias effectively. In one, researchers Andreas Leibbrandt and John A. List posted two versions of announcements for administrative assistant jobs in stereotypically masculine businesses—NASCAR, football, and basketball. One version said nothing about salary; the other said "salary negotiable." Leibbrandt and List wanted to investigate the well-documented phenomenon that women are less likely to negotiate their salaries than men, which contributes to the pay gap between the sexes. Could a simple two-word phrase interrupt that pattern?

It could. In fact, not only did the "salary negotiable" language close the negotiation gap between men and women, it closed the pay gap between the male and female hires by 45%.

This experimental approach is a classic example of a bias interrupter: It changed the basic business system in a way that stopped a

Idea in Brief

The Challenge

The technology industry has a well-documented diversity problem. But previous efforts to fix it—through sweeping cultural change initiatives or well-intentioned mentoring programs—have failed.

The Analysis

Biases that hold women back include prove-it-again!, the tightrope, the maternal wall, and the tug-of-war. Forty years of social science research have shown that biases like these will persist unless they are interrupted.

The Solution

Leaders need to design "bias interrupters"—changes to essential talent management systems that stop patterns of bias in their tracks. By redesigning how rewards and assignments are handled, managers can be sure they're retaining their best and brightest.

pattern of bias in its tracks. And it did so without talking about bias at all (or even raising it). It also highlights three advantages that bias interrupters have over the sweeping cultural change initiatives that researchers who study organizational bias tend to recommend. Such efforts can be effective, but they're expensive—and often abandoned when a new CEO arrives with different priorities. Recently, for instance, Best Buy's new CEO eliminated the company's much-ballyhooed Results Only Work Environment, despite rigorous data documenting its business benefits.

First, bias interrupters are based on objective metrics, whereas cultural initiatives tend to rely on earnest conversations. Second, interrupters are iterative, so they allow companies to try small interventions and then scale them up. Last, interrupters build change into the basic business systems that perpetuate bias, so they are less likely to disappear when a new CEO decides that diversity is not an imperative.

While the evidence of the effectiveness of interrupters is growing in social science literature, the effort to systematically pilot and test them in companies is just beginning. I've started to work with several companies, including Twitter and the Silicon Valley law firm Fenwick & West, on a model for building bias interrupters. With Jennifer Berdahl from the University of British Columbia, I'm also forming a working group to explore interrupters with other social scientists. It's still early days, but here's the approach I'm using to help companies identify, measure, and address diversity-related bias.

Step #1: Determine Whether There's a Problem

The first step is to find out whether women in your organization are encountering one or more of the four basic patterns of gender bias. Here's a quick primer:

Prove-it-again!

Women often have to provide more evidence of competence than men do to be seen as equally capable, a problem documented in scores of studies on double standards, attribution bias, leniency bias, recall bias, and polarized evaluations. About two-thirds of the 127 professional women that I and Erika Hall, now a professor at Emory's Goizueta Business School, interviewed for the book *What Works for Women at Work* reported prove-it-again problems. Our interviews additionally suggested that women in tech often get promoted but don't get the title or salary that typically accompanies the new job, and that women's technical expertise is dismissed the minute they are no longer in technical roles. "We're constantly asked 'if you write any code' when speaking about technical topics and giving technical presentations, despite just having given a talk on writing code," note the authors of the widely circulated "Open Letter on Feminism in Tech."

Tightrope

This is the kind of bias faced by the female salary negotiators. High-status jobs are seen as requiring stereotypically masculine qualities, while women are expected to be modest and self-effacing, so women must walk a tightrope between being seen as too feminine to be effective and too masculine to be likable. Nearly three-fourths of the women we interviewed reported tightrope issues, with twice as many reports of "too feminine" as "too masculine" problems. Classic "too feminine" problems are large

"Housework" vs. "Glamour Work"

IN MANY COMPANIES, WOMEN ARE expected to do disproportionate amounts of "housework," which includes both domestic tasks, like planning parties, and undervalued tasks, such as those listed below.

Industry	Housework	Glamour work
High tech	Managing projects	Writing the code
Law firms	Being a "service partner" who does the actual legal work	Bringing in clients
Consulting	Managing projects, delivering work, mentoring colleagues	Developing new business, managing C-suite relationships, serving as subject matter experts
Investment management firms	Handling logistics on pitches, working for low-profile clients	Making investment decisions, executing high-profile deals, managing key client relationships
Academia	Being dean of students or on the admissions committee	Publishing in prestigious journals
Architecture	Detailing bathrooms and elevators	Visiting sites, pitching to clients, being the lead in design competitions
Surgery	Managing patient care outside the operating room	Performing surgeries
Science	Organizing and executing lab work	Strategic planning of future research direction, publishing in prestigious journals

loads of "office housework"—which includes fetching documents, planning parties and conferences, and cleaning up messes, literally and figuratively—and assignments to do undervalued tasks. In tech, power and prestige lie with those who "own the code"; even very talented women end up in marketing or project management roles instead. Yet a woman risks being seen as "not a team player" if she turns away work that men are rarely asked to do. (See the sidebar "'Housework' vs. 'Glamour Work.'")

In addition, when women are direct, outspoken, competitive, or assertive—rather than "nice"—they often face a backlash, including what one researcher called "the sexual harassment of uppity women" in a study showing that dominant women actually experience the most harassment. There's an avalanche of sexual harassment in tech, ranging from "angry e-mails that threaten us to leave the industry, because 'it doesn't need any more c***s ruining it'" to "booth babes" and networking events held in strip clubs. This "brogrammer" culture has pushed many women out of the field. In 1985, 37% of computer science degrees were awarded to women; in 2012 only 18% were. In 1991 women held 37% of all computing jobs; today they hold only 26%. Forty-one percent of women leave tech companies after 10 years, as opposed to 17% of men.

Maternal wall

Bias triggered by motherhood has dramatic effects. In one famous study subjects evaluated pairs of equally qualified candidates, one of whom was a mother. The subjects received identical résumés, but the candidate who was a mother varied. The researchers found that mothers were 79% less likely to be hired, half as likely to be promoted, offered an average of $11,000 less in salary, and held to higher performance and punctuality standards. Another study looked at mothers who were considered indisputably competent and committed. Because of their dedication to the job, they were seen as bad mothers and bad people. As a result, they were disliked and held to higher performance standards.

A common take is that the long-hours culture drives mothers out of tech, but often what drives them out is sexism. As one woman told me, "Women. . .29, 30. . .were hitting the glass ceiling that I've been hitting for a long time. And if they could [afford to]. . ., they would just start having babies and drop out because they wanted to have kids anyway, and it's hard to show up every day and fight and fight and fight." While many women in tech have praised the industry for allowing flexible hours and remote working arrangements, mothers remain suspect. Take the recent flap when Marissa Mayer, the CEO of Yahoo, was late to a meeting. The only reason that story made the news is that it confirmed the stereotype that mothers aren't suited to be CEOs. Fifty-nine percent of the mothers Hall and I interviewed reported experiencing maternal wall bias.

Tug-of-war

This pattern, reported by 45% of the women interviewed, occurs when gender bias against women fuels conflict among women. Research shows that women who encounter discrimination early in their careers tend to distance themselves from other women, refuse to help them, or even align themselves with men at other women's expense. Distancing oneself from complaints against sexism becomes an emblem of loyalty. "I'm not a girl at Google; I'm a geek at Google," was Marissa Mayer's standard response to questions about what it was like being one of the few female programmers at the company. Today, when asked how we can encourage more women to become engineers, Mayer responds that her focus is getting more men and women to become engineers. The Open Letter protests that its authors have been "paraded around by men in the industry for how nice we've been in trying to address the social problems in tech as a way to discredit more vocal, astutely firm feminist voices. We don't like this, we've never liked it, and it needs to stop."

Organizations need to find out how, if at all, these four patterns affect women's careers internally. A good place to start is with confidential interviews or focus groups conducted by an expert in the patterns of bias. Obviously, the people in a focus group have to trust one another not to disclose who said what. One organization I'm working with has so few women that they all know one another—and already agree that there's a problem. The idea that the women in their company already discuss these issues freely with one another often surprises male senior executives—and so do the focus group results.

Step #2: Identify Key Metrics

Your internal research will often bring to light ways to measure the problem, which you can use to identify a baseline and track the results of changes. In one organization in which internal referrals play a major role, women suggested an elegant metric: Ask both men and women if they got their last five opportunities from inside or outside the firm. In this organization and many others, senior men typically staff their teams with people they feel comfortable with—people like themselves. (It's called "in-group favoritism.") Assumptions that "men have families to support" and that "mothers do not want stretch assignments" also play a role; examining how assignments are distributed can surface some of these.

If the problem's office housework, the metric will be different. One organization that identified this as a major issue proposed setting up a list of low-profile tasks (List A) and high-profile ones (List B). The plan was to ask men and women what percentage of their time was spent on tasks from List A versus List B.

With maternal wall bias, it's key to track how women's assignments differ before and after maternity leaves. At the Center for WorkLife Law, which I direct, we frequently hear that women returning from maternity leave get fewer or poor-quality assignments. (The result, of course, is that they quit.)

The right metrics will differ from organization to organization, depending on the types of bias uncovered and the strategic goals of the firm. But it does make sense to be systematic. Any firm undertaking this work should think carefully about four processes: how people are hired, how work is assigned, what happens during performance evaluations, and how compensation is determined. In addition, it should look for cultural markers that exclude outsiders. In tech, that's the oft-celebrated "brogrammer" culture. Companies should go beyond the classic "body counts," which simply note the number of women but don't tell you why women didn't get hired, why they don't get promoted, or why they leave sooner than you want them to (if they do).

Step #3: Experiment, Measure Success—and Keep Trying

Once you've assessed bias and identified key metrics, the next step is to interrupt the bias, see whether the metrics improve, and then—if no improvement occurs—ratchet up to stronger interventions. The ideal interrupter is like the one in the Leibbrandt/List experiment: easy to do and not requiring training on, or even a discussion of, gender bias.

Another good example of a successful interrupter comes from Google. The company's analytics showed that women were being promoted less often than men because, to be promoted at Google, you needed to nominate yourself. Fewer women did so, presumably because modesty is so associated with femininity that women who advocated for themselves often encountered pushback, just as with negotiation. Google's response was to include female leaders at workshops on when and how to put yourself forward. This signaled to women that they were expected to self-promote. So they did, and the gender difference among Googlers nominating themselves all but disappeared.

One organization I've spoken with is concerned about whether gender bias is affecting performance evaluations. The Center for WorkLife Law proposed reading its performance evaluations to spot patterns of bias. The company's executives sensibly suggested starting off with a staff meeting explaining that they're committed to improving the quality of performance evaluations, and introducing the four patterns. Great idea: Accountability causes more people to interrupt automatic bias more often.

What happens if you find bias—how should you present it to the people involved in the relevant processes? Obviously, it's important to design feedback loops very carefully, so people don't feel they are on a forced march into political correctness. Just as the metrics and the interrupters will differ from firm to firm, so will the feedback loops. But the best tone is judgment free and evidence based: "I'll bet you're not aware that there's an inconsistency in the way you're evaluating women and men; here's a study that explains why this is common."

Where should companies begin experimenting? Again, by looking at the same core processes they examined in Step 2. Though research on and experiments with interrupters are relatively new, they suggest the following brief template:

Hiring

Develop job-advertisement guidelines that advise steering clear of masculine-gendered words like "competitive," "assertive," and "ambitious." Track whether those guidelines are followed. To the extent possible, give hiring managers blinded résumés, so they can't tell whether the applicant is a man or a woman. Track whether this practice changes hiring numbers. Agree in advance on standard interview questions, watch for subtle biases, and adjust the list of questions as you learn which ones work well for all candidates. A seemingly harmless question like "Tell me about a personal or professional accomplishment that best shows your strengths" can be problematic. Since women are wary of bragging (the tightrope problem), they'll often answer this question by telling you how proud they are of their kids (women are allowed to brag about their children); men will give a work-related answer and advance their cause more effectively.

Assignments

The gentlest interrupter is one that documents that men and women are getting different kinds of projects and offers a training on how the four patterns of bias commonly affect assignments. If that doesn't work, more robust interventions are needed, up to and including a formal assignment system. As Louise Roth points out in her study of high finance, a huge problem is the channeling of women into groups with lower revenue potential. "These firms develop mathematical models for all sorts of other things," says Roth, "so why not for dividing work evenly?"

Performance evaluations

Having someone who is trained in the literature on gender bias read through all performance evaluations, which Ernst & Young has done for years, can help if your analysis shows that bias is affecting them. Be sure to track whether praise differentially translates into high overall evaluations for men but not women. Check, too, whether similar evaluations translate into greater rewards for men than for women.

Promotion and compensation

Systems that require people to brag will push women out onto the tightrope—disliked but respected if they do, and liked but not respected if they don't. In fact, any hiring, evaluation, or other

The Research

THIS WORK GROWS OUT OF the research I did for *What Works for Women at Work: Four Patterns Working Women Need to Know* (cowritten with my daughter Rachel Dempsey), which examined whether the kinds of gender bias documented in social psychology labs shows up in real workplaces. My team interviewed 127 professional women, including 63 in science, technology, math, and engineering, and 71 women of color. Our finding: Virtually all the women interviewed (96%) reported experiencing one or more of the patterns documented in experimental studies. Only five women had not, and three of them had founded their own companies.

process that requires self-promotion should take a hint from the Leibbrandt/List experiment and the Google example. Self-promotion should be cabined into formal contexts in which both men and women are sent the message that everyone is expected to tout his or her accomplishments.

Compensation systems based on objective metrics that are not easy to game offer a strong control on gender bias and give managers insight into who their most valuable players actually are. Roth's study of bankers confirmed what I've also found: Women fare best in jobs where performance is measured by objective metrics. Objectivity often suffers, however, when compensation is set by a powerful group of insiders. Law firm compensation systems, in which pay depends heavily on backroom negotiations over credit for bringing in clients, are a petri dish for bias. In a 2010 study about 30% of women in law firms reported being bullied out of receiving such credit.

The promise of bias interrupters is that they allow for institutional learning and build on a critical, consistent finding: Doing anything once will not change organizational culture forever. You need to continually interrupt bias. And you need to be empirical: Keep throwing spaghetti at the wall until some sticks. Tech companies are used to spaghetti flinging, which makes them a perfect fit for an iterative process rather than one grand gesture.

What a company can't do is establish metrics, document bias, and then do nothing. That's a recipe for legal liability. But as long as companies that find bias try in good faith to remedy it, interrupters promise to be both more effective, and probably cheaper, than elaborate cultural change initiatives. And they will work a whole lot better than the other standard tools of the diversity industrial complex. Unlike women's initiatives, which often seek to fix women, and unlike stand-alone bias training, which can make diversity metrics worse, interrupters do something novel. They identify how bias is playing out in real time. And then they short-circuit it.

Originally published in October 2014. Reprint R1410H

Why Men Still Get More Promotions Than Women

by Herminia Ibarra, Nancy M. Carter, and Christine Silva

NATHALIE (ALL NAMES IN THIS article are disguised), a senior marketing manager at a multinational consumer goods company and a contender for chairman in her country, was advised by her boss to raise her profile locally. An excellent intracompany network wouldn't be enough to land her the new role, he told her; she must also become active in events and associations in her region. Recently matched with a high-level mentor through a companywide program, she had barely completed the lengthy prework assigned for that when she received an invitation to an exclusive executive-training program for high potentials—for which she was asked to fill out more self-assessments and career-planning documents. "I'd been here for 12 years, and nothing happened," observes Nathalie. "Now I am being mentored to death."

Amy, a midlevel sales manager for the same firm, struggles with a similar problem: "My mentor's idea of a development plan is how many external and internal meetings I can get exposure to, what presentations I can go to and deliver, and what meetings I can travel to," she says. "I just hate these things that add work. I hate to say it, but I am so busy. I have three kids. On top of that, what my current boss really wants me to do is to focus on 'breakthrough thinking,' and I agree. I am going to be in a wheelchair by the time I get to be vice president, because they are going to drill me into the ground with all these extra-credit projects."

With turnover sky-high in the company's fast-growing Chinese market, Julie, a much-valued finance manager with growth potential, has likewise undergone intensive mentoring—and she worries that she may be getting caught betwixt and between. When she was nominated for a high-potential program, her boss complained that the corporate team was interfering with the mentoring operation he was already running in the region. Julie also took part in a less formal scheme pairing junior and senior finance leaders. "I'd prefer to be involved in the corporate program because it is more high-profile," says Julie, "but it all adds up to a lot of mentoring."

Nathalie, Amy, and Julie are not atypical. As companies continue to see their pipelines leak at mid-to-senior levels even though they've invested considerable time and resources in mentors and developmental opportunities, they are actively searching for ways to retain their best female talent. In a 2010 World Economic Forum report on corporate practices for gender diversity in 20 countries, 59% of the companies surveyed say they offer internally led mentoring and networking programs, and 28% say they have women-specific programs. But does all this effort translate into actual promotions and appointments for both sexes?

The numbers suggest not. A 2008 Catalyst survey of more than 4,000 full-time-employed men and women—high potentials who graduated from top MBA programs worldwide from 1996 to 2007—shows that the women are paid $4,600 less in their first post-MBA jobs, occupy lower-level management positions, and have significantly less career satisfaction than their male counterparts with the same education. That's also the case when we take into account factors such as their industry, prior work experience, aspirations, and whether they have children. (For more findings, see Nancy M. Carter and Christine Silva, "Women

Idea in Brief

Although women are mentored, they're not being promoted. A Catalyst study of more than 4,000 high potentials shows that more women than men have mentors—yet women are *less* likely to advance in their careers. That's because they're not actively sponsored the way the men are.

Sponsors go beyond giving feedback and advice; they advocate for their mentees and help them gain visibility in the company. They fight to get their protégés to the next level.

Organizations such as Deutsche Bank, Unilever, Sodexo, and IBM Europe have established sponsorship programs to facilitate the promotion of high-potential women. Programs that get results clarify and communicate goals, match sponsors and mentees on the basis of those goals, coordinate corporate and regional efforts, train sponsors, and hold sponsors accountable.

in Management: Delusions of Progress," HBR March 2010.) Yet among that same group, more women than men report having mentors. If the women are being mentored so thoroughly, why aren't they moving into higher management positions?

To better understand what is going on, we conducted in-depth interviews with 40 high-potential men and women (including Nathalie, Amy, and Julie) who were selected by their large multinational company to participate in its high-level mentoring program. We asked about the hurdles they've faced as they've moved into more-senior roles, as well as what kinds of help and support they've received for their transitions. We also analyzed the 2008 survey to uncover any differences in how men and women are mentored and in the effects of their mentoring on advancement. Last, we compared those data with the results of a 2010 survey of the same population, in which we asked participants to report on promotions and lateral moves since 2008.

All mentoring is not created equal, we discovered. There is a special kind of relationship—called sponsorship—in which the mentor goes beyond giving feedback and advice and uses his or her influence with senior executives to advocate for the mentee.

Our interviews and surveys alike suggest that high-potential women are overmentored and undersponsored relative to their male peers—and that they are not advancing in their organizations. Furthermore, without sponsorship, women not only are less likely than men to be appointed to top roles but may also be more reluctant to go for them.

Why Mentoring Fails Women

Although more women than men in the 2008 Catalyst survey report having mentors, the women's mentors have less organizational clout. We find this to be true even after controlling for the fact that women start in lower-level positions post-MBA. That's a real disadvantage, the study shows, because the more senior the mentor, the faster the mentee's career advancement. Despite all the effort that has gone into developing the women since 2008, the follow-up survey in 2010 reveals that the men have received 15% more promotions. The two groups have had similar numbers of lateral moves (same-level job assignments in different functions, designed to give high potentials exposure to various parts of the business). But men were receiving promotions after the lateral moves; for the women, the moves were offered in lieu of advancement.

Of course, the ultimate test of the power of mentoring would be to show that its presence during the 2008 survey is a statistically significant predictor of promotion by the time of the 2010 survey. That's true for the men but not for the women. Though women may be getting support and guidance, mentoring relationships aren't leading to nearly as many promotions for them as for men.

The survey findings are echoed in our interviews: Men and women alike say they get valuable career advice from their mentors, but it's mostly men who describe being sponsored. Many women explain how mentoring relationships have helped them understand themselves, their preferred styles of operating, and ways they might need to change as they move up the leadership pipeline. By contrast, men tell stories about how their bosses and informal mentors

Are Women as Likely as Men to Get Mentoring? Yes.

THEY'RE ACTUALLY MORE SO: In the 2008 Catalyst survey, **83%** of women and 76% of men say they've had at least one mentor at some point in their careers. Indeed, 21% of women say they've had four or more mentors, compared with 15% of men.

Does Mentoring Provide the Same Career Benefits to Men and Women? No.

AMONG SURVEY PARTICIPANTS WHO HAD active mentoring relationships in 2008, fully **72%** of the men had received one or more promotions by 2010, compared with 65% of the women.

Do Men and Women Have the Same Kinds of Mentors? No.

IN 2008, 78% OF MEN were actively mentored by a CEO or another senior executive, compared with 69% of women.

More women than men had junior-level mentors: **7%** of women were mentored by a nonmanager or a first-level manager, compared with 4% of men.

Though both groups had more male than female mentors on balance, **36%** of women had female mentors, whereas only 11% of men did.

Do Men and Women Get Their Mentors in the Same Way? Yes.

MOST MEN AND WOMEN—67% of the groups combined—found their mentors on their own, relying on personal networks. Just **18%** of women and 16% of men formed their mentoring relationships with the help of formal programs.

Does Having Formal Versus Informal Mentoring Make Any Difference in Terms of Promotions? Yes.

WOMEN WHO HAD FOUND MENTORS through formal programs had received more promotions by 2010 than women who had found mentors on their own (by a ratio of almost three to two).

Among all participants who had found mentors on their own, the men received more promotions than the women (again, by a ratio of almost three to two).

For more on how companies are providing sponsorship, go to www.catalyst.org/publication/413/mentoring-sponsorship.

have helped them plan their moves and take charge in new roles, in addition to endorsing their authority publicly. As one male mentee recounts, in a typical comment:

"My boss said, 'You are ready for a general management job. You can do it. Now we need to find you a job: What are the tricks we need to figure out? You have to talk to this person and to that one and that one.' They are all executive committee members. My boss was a network type of a person. . . . Before he left, he put me in touch with the head of supply chain, which is how I managed to get this job."

Not only do the women report few examples of this kind of endorsement; they also share numerous stories about how they've had to fight with their mentors to be viewed as ready for the next role.

Paradoxically, just when women are most likely to need sponsorship—as they shoot for the highest-level jobs—they may be least likely to get it. Women are still perceived as "risky" appointments for such roles by often male-dominated committees. In a study of top-performing CEOs, for instance, the women were nearly twice as likely as the men to have been hired from outside the company (see Morten T. Hansen, Herminia Ibarra, and Urs Peyer, "The Best-Performing CEOs in the World," HBR January–February 2010). That finding suggests that women are less likely to emerge as winners in their firms' own CEO tournaments.

Sponsorship That Works

Impatient with the speed at which women are reaching the top levels, many leading-edge companies we work with are converging on a new set of strategies to ensure that high-potential women are sponsored for the most-senior posts. Those principles can make all the difference between a sponsorship program that gets results and one that simply looks great on paper.

Clarify and communicate the intent of the program

It's hard to do a good job of both mentoring and sponsoring within the same program. Often the best mentors—those who provide caring and altruistic advice and counseling—are not the highfliers who have the influence to pull people up through the system. Employees expecting one form of support can be very disappointed when they get the other. And companies hoping to do A can find themselves with a program that instead does B. To prevent such problems, they need to clearly define what they're trying to accomplish.

Mentors and Sponsors: How They Differ

COMPANIES NEED TO MAKE A sharper distinction between mentoring and sponsorship. Mentors offer "psychosocial" support for personal and professional development, plus career help that includes advice and coaching, as Boston University's Kathy Kram explains in her pioneering research. Only sponsors actively advocate for advancement.

"Classical mentoring" (ideal but rare) combines psychosocial and career support. Usually, though, workers get one or the other—or if they get both, it's from different sources.

Analysis of hundreds of studies shows that people derive more satisfaction from mentoring but need sponsorship. Without sponsorship, a person is likely to be overlooked for promotion, regardless of his or her competence and performance—particularly at mid-career and beyond, when competition for promotions increases.

Mentors

- Can sit at any level in the hierarchy
- Provide emotional support, feedback on how to improve, and other advice
- Serve as role models
- Help mentees learn to navigate corporate politics
- Strive to increase mentees' sense of competence and self-worth
- Focus on mentees' personal and professional development

Sponsors

- Must be senior managers with influence
- Give protégés exposure to other executives who may help their careers
- Make sure their people are considered for promising opportunities and challenging assignments
- Protect their protégés from negative publicity or damaging contact with senior executives
- Fight to get their people promoted

At Deutsche Bank, for example, internal research revealed that female managing directors who left the firm to work for competitors were not doing so to improve their work/life balance. Rather, they'd been offered bigger jobs externally, ones they weren't considered for internally. Deutsche Bank responded by creating a sponsorship program aimed at assigning more women to critical posts. It paired mentees with executive committee members to increase the female talent pool's exposure to the committee and ensure that the women had influential advocates for promotion. Now, one-third of the participants are in larger roles than they were in a year ago, and another third are deemed ready by senior management and HR to take on broader responsibilities.

Select and match sponsors and high-potential women in light of program goals

When the objective of a program is career advancement for high potentials, mentors and sponsors are typically selected on the basis of position power. When the goal is personal development, matches are made to increase the likelihood of frequent contact and good chemistry.

Unilever has established a program with the explicit objective of promoting more high-potential women to the firm's most-senior levels. The two key criteria for selecting the sponsors, all members of Unilever's senior ranks, are experience in areas where the high potentials have developmental gaps, and presence at the table when the appointment decisions get made. Given the company's international scope and matrix organization, this means that many of the women do not live and work in the same location as their sponsors. So some don't spend much face-to-face time with sponsors, but they do have advocates at promotion time.

Coordinate efforts and involve direct supervisors

Centrally run mentoring programs that sidestep direct bosses can inadvertently communicate that diversity is an HR problem that requires no effort from the front lines.

Coordination of corporate and local efforts is especially important when it comes to senior-level participants in whom companies invest significantly. Effective sponsorship does not stand alone but is one facet of a comprehensive program that includes performance evaluation, training and development, and succession planning—all of which add up to more than the sum of the parts. The Deutsche Bank sponsorship program for female managing directors, for instance, is one piece of a highly tailored initiative that also involves leadership evaluations, external coaches, and leadership workshops.

Train sponsors on the complexities of gender and leadership
Good sponsorship requires a set of skills and sensibilities that most companies' star executives do not necessarily possess. When you layer on top some of the complexities of sponsor relationships between senior men and junior women, you easily have a recipe for misunderstanding. The strategies and tactics that helped the men progress in their careers may not be appealing or even feasible for the women.

A classic case is the challenge of developing a credible leadership style in a context where most of the successful role models are male. One of the women in our research describes the problem like this: "My mentor advised me that I should pay more attention to my strategic influencing skills. . .but often he suggests I do things that totally contradict my personality." The behavioral styles that are most valued in traditionally masculine cultures—and most used as indicators of "potential"—are often unappealing or unnatural for high-potential women, whose sense of authenticity can feel violated by the tacit leadership requirements.

A further complexity is the famed "double bind" examined in Alice H. Eagly and Linda L. Carli's book *Through the Labyrinth* (Harvard Business Review Press, 2007) and in the 2007 Catalyst research report "The Double-Bind Dilemma for Women in Leadership." Here's the problem, in short: The assertive, authoritative, dominant behaviors that people associate with leadership are frequently deemed less attractive in women. Male mentors who have never faced this dilemma themselves may be hard-pressed to provide useful advice. As one of our interview participants describes, even well-intended mentors have trouble helping women navigate the fine line between being "not aggressive enough" or "lacking in presence" and being "too aggressive" or "too controlling." She explains the challenge of dealing with conflicting expectations from two different bosses:

"My old boss told me, 'If you want to move up, you have to change your style. You are too brutal, too demanding, too tough, too clear, and not participative enough.' My new boss is different: He drives performance, values speed. Now I am told, 'You have to be more demanding.' I was really working on being more indirect, but now I will try to combine the best of both."

Male sponsors can be taught to recognize such gender-related dilemmas. Women in Sodexo's reciprocal-mentoring program, for example, have been promoted at higher rates than other high-potential women at the company, in part because the senior male mentors serve as career sponsors and (thanks to the upward mentoring) learn to manage their unconscious biases.

Hold sponsors accountable

To fully reap the benefits of sponsorship, companies must hold sponsors accountable. At IBM Europe, a sponsorship program designed for senior women below the executive level aims to promote selected participants within one year. Sponsors, all vice presidents or general managers, are charged with making sure that participants are indeed ready within a year. So they work hard to raise the women's profiles, talk up the candidates to decision makers, and find the high potentials internal projects that will fill in their skills gaps and make them promotable. Failure to obtain a promotion is viewed as a failure of the sponsor, not of the candidate.

Although our data show that formal programs can be quite effective in getting women promoted, a potential pitfall is their fixed duration. Sponsors typically declare victory and move on after their high potentials advance—just when they need help to successfully take charge in their new roles. We know of no programs designed to shore up participants past promotion and through the "first 100 days" in the new position. With that extra bit of attention, sponsors could help deliver not just promotions but strong transitions.

Although the women we interviewed all come from the same company, the trends there mirror those at many other firms we've worked with and observed. And the survey responses, gathered from men and women at hundreds of firms, also provide strong evidence for gender difference in mentoring outcomes.

More sponsoring may lead to more and faster promotions for women, but it is not a magic bullet: There is still much to do to close the gap between men's and women's advancement. Some improvements—such as supportive bosses and inclusive cultures— are a lot harder to mandate than formal mentoring programs but essential if those programs are to have their intended effects. Clearly, however, the critical first step is to stop overmentoring and start accountable sponsoring for both sexes.

Originally published in September 2010. Reprint R1009F

When No One Retires

by Paul Irving

BEFORE OUR EYES, THE WORLD is undergoing a massive demographic transformation. In many countries, the population is getting old. Very old. Globally, the number of people age 60 and over is projected to double to more than 2 billion by 2050 and those 60 and over will outnumber children under the age of 5. In the United States, about 10,000 people turn 65 each day, and one in five Americans will be 65 or older by 2030. By 2035, Americans of retirement age will eclipse the number of people aged 18 and under for the first time in U.S. history.

The reasons for this age shift are many—medical advances that keep people healthier longer, dropping fertility rates, and so on—but the net result is the same: Populations around the world will look very different in the decades ahead.

Some in the public and private sector are already taking note—and sounding the alarm. In his first term as chairman of the U.S. Federal Reserve, with the Great Recession looming, Ben Bernanke remarked, "In the coming decades, many forces will shape our economy and our society, but in all likelihood no single factor will have as pervasive an effect as the aging of our population." Back in 2010, Standard & Poor's predicted that the biggest influence on "the future of national economic health, public finances, and policymaking" will be "the irreversible rate at which the world's population is aging."

The world is getting older

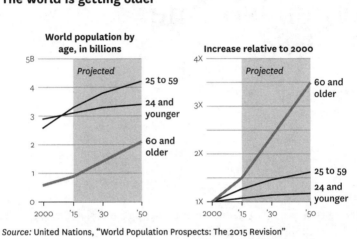

Source: United Nations, "World Population Prospects: The 2015 Revision"

This societal shift will undoubtedly change work, too: More and more Americans want to work longer—or have to, given that many aren't saving adequately for retirement. Soon, the workforce will include people from as many as five generations ranging in age from teenagers to 80-somethings.

Are companies prepared? The short answer is "no." Aging will affect every aspect of business operations—whether it's talent recruitment, the structure of compensation and benefits, the development of products and services, how innovation is unlocked, how offices and factories are designed, and even how work is structured—but for some reason, the message just hasn't gotten through. In general, corporate leaders have yet to invest the time and resources necessary to fully grasp the unprecedented ways that aging will change the rules of the game.

What's more, those who *do* think about the impacts of an aging population typically see a looming crisis—not an opportunity. They fail to appreciate the potential that older adults present as workers and consumers. The reality, however, is that increasing longevity contributes to global economic growth. Today's older adults

Idea in Brief

Before our eyes, the world is undergoing a massive demographic transformation. In many countries, the population is aging rapidly. In the United States, about 10,000 people turn 65 each day, and one in five Americans will be 65 or older by 2030. This societal shift will affect every aspect of business operations, but corporate leaders have not yet grasped the unprecedented ways that an aging workforce will change the rules of the game. Those who *do* think about the impacts typically see a looming crisis—not an opportunity. This article helps companies develop a "longevity strategy" for fostering a vibrant multigenerational workforce.

are generally healthier and more active than those of generations past, and they are changing the nature of retirement as they continue to learn, work, and contribute. In the workplace, they provide emotional stability, complex problem-solving skills, nuanced thinking, and institutional know-how. Their talents complement those of younger workers, and their guidance and support enhance performance and intergenerational collaboration. In encore careers, volunteering, and civic and social settings, their experience and problem-solving abilities contribute to society's well-being.

In the public sector, policy makers are beginning to take action. Efforts are under way in the United States to reimagine communities to enhance "age friendliness," develop strategies to improve infrastructure, enhance wellness and disease prevention, and design new ways to invest for retirement as traditional income sources like pensions and defined benefit plans dry up. But such efforts are still early stage, and given the slow pace of governmental change they will likely take years to evolve.

Companies, by contrast, are uniquely positioned to change practices and attitudes *now*. Transformation won't be easy, but companies that move past today's preconceptions about older employees and respond and adapt to changing demographics will realize significant dividends, generating new possibilities for financial return and enhancing the lives of their employees and customers. I spent many years in executive management, corporate law, and board service.

Based on this experience, along with research conducted with Arielle Burstein, Kevin Proff, and other members of our staff at the Milken Institute Center for the Future of Aging, I have developed a framework for building a "longevity strategy" that companies can use to create a vibrant multigenerational workforce. Broadly, a longevity strategy should include two key elements: internal-facing activities (hiring, retention, and mining the talents of workers of all ages) and external-facing ones (how your company positions itself and its products and services to customers and stakeholders). In this article, I'll address the internal activities companies should be engaging in.

But first, let's examine why leaders seem to be overlooking the opportunities of an aging population.

The Ageism Effect

There's broad consensus that the global population is changing and growing significantly older. There's also a prevailing opinion that the impacts on society will largely be negative. A Government Accountability Office report warns that older populations will bring slower growth, lower productivity, and increasing dependency on society. A report from the Congressional Budget Office projects that higher entitlement costs associated with an aging population will drive up expenses relative to revenues, increasing the federal deficit. The World Bank foresees fading potential in economies across the globe, warning in 2018 of "headwinds from ageing populations in both advanced and developing economies, expecting decreased labour supply and productivity growth." Such predictions serve to further entrench the belief that older workers are an expensive drag on society.

What's at the heart of this gloomy outlook? Economists often refer to what's known as the dependency ratio: the number of people not typically in the workforce—those younger than 15 and older than 65—in a population divided by the number of working-age people. This measure assumes that older adults are generally unproductive and can be expected to do little other than consume benefits in their later years. Serious concerns about the so-called "silver tsunami" are justified if this assumption is correct: The prospect of a massive

The global aging phenomenon

Projected breakdown of world population, by region

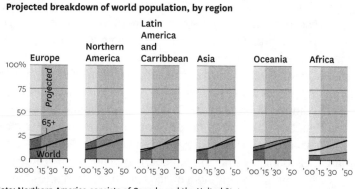

Note: Northern America consists of Canada and the United States.
Source: United Nations, "World Population Prospects: The 2015 Revision"

population of sick, disengaged, lonely, needy, and cognitively impaired people is a dark one indeed.

This picture, however, is simply not accurate. While some older adults do suffer from disabling physical and cognitive conditions or are otherwise unable to maintain an active lifestyle, far more are able and inclined to stay in the game longer, disproving assumptions about their prospects for work and productivity. The work of Laura Carstensen and her colleagues at the Stanford Center on Longevity shows that typical 60-something workers today are healthy, experienced, and more likely than younger colleagues to be satisfied with their jobs. They have a strong work ethic and loyalty to their employers. They are motivated, knowledgeable, adept at resolving social dilemmas, and care more about meaningful contributions and less about self-advancement. They are more likely than their younger counterparts to build social cohesion and to share information and organizational values.

Yet the flawed perceptions persist, a byproduct of stubborn and pervasive ageism. Positive attributes of older workers are crowded out by negative stereotypes that infect work settings and devalue older adults in a youth-oriented culture. Older adults regularly find themselves on the losing end of hiring decisions, promotions, and even volunteer opportunities. Research from AARP found that approximately two-thirds of workers ages 45 to 74 said they have seen or experienced age discrimination in the workplace. Of those, a remarkable 92% said age discrimination is very, or somewhat, common. Research for the Federal Reserve Bank of San Francisco backs this up. A study involving 40,000 made-up résumés found compelling evidence that older applicants, especially women, suffer consistent age discrimination. A case in point is IBM, which is currently facing allegations of using improper practices to marginalize and terminate older workers.

There's more: Deloitte's 2018 Global Human Capital Trends study found that 20% of business and HR leaders surveyed viewed older workers as a competitive disadvantage and an impediment to the progress of younger workers. The report concludes that "there may be a significant hidden problem of age bias in the workforce today." It also warns that "left unaddressed, perceptions that a company's culture and employment practices suffer from age bias could damage its brand and social capital."

The negative cultural overlay about aging is reinforced by media and advertising that often portray older adults in clichéd, patronizing ways. A classic example is Life Alert's ad from the 1980s for its medical alert necklace, immortalizing the phrase "I've fallen, and I can't get up!" Recent ads by E*TRADE and Postmates have also drawn criticism as ageist. A more subtle, but just as damaging example is the trumpeting of "anti-aging" benefits on beauty products as a marketing tool, suggesting that growing older is, by definition, a negative process.

Some companies are pushing back: In a recent video, T-Mobile's John Legere took on the topic of ageist stereotypes while promoting a T-Mobile service for adults age 55-plus. He chided competitors for what he called their belittling treatment of older adults in marketing campaigns that emphasize large-size phone buttons and imply that boomers are tech idiots. "Degrading at the highest level," Legere calls it. "The carriers assume boomers are a bunch of old people stuck in the past who can't figure out how the internet works. News flash, carriers: Boomers invented the internet."

Yet for the most part, employers continue to invest far more in young employees and generally do not train workers over 50. In fact, many companies would rather not think about the existence of older workers all. "Today it is socially unacceptable to ignore, ridicule, or stereotype someone based on their gender, race, or sexual orientation," points out Jo Ann Jenkins, the CEO of AARP. "So why is it still acceptable to do this to people based on their age?"

Over the past decades, companies have recognized the economic and social benefits of women, people of color, and LGBT individuals in the workforce. These priority initiatives must be continued—obviously, we're not even close to achieving genuine equality in the corporate world; at the same time, the inclusion of older adults in the business diversity matrix is long overdue. Patricia Milligan, senior partner and global leader for Mercer's Multinational Client Group, observes, "At the most respected multinational companies, the single class not represented from a diversity and inclusion perspective is older workers. LGBT, racial and ethnic diversity, women, people with physical disabilities, veterans—you can find an affinity group in a corporation for everything, except an older worker."

The U.S. labor force is getting older, too

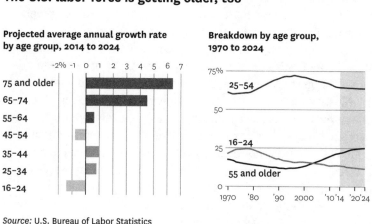

Projected average annual growth rate by age group, 2014 to 2024

Breakdown by age group, 1970 to 2024

Source: U.S. Bureau of Labor Statistics

Managing a Multigenerational Workforce

How can companies push past stereotypes and other organizational impediments to tap into a thriving and talented population of older workers? A range of best practices have been emerging and some companies are making real progress. Each points to specific changes companies should be considering as they develop their own strategies.

Redefine the workweek

To start, you need to reconsider the out-of-date idea that all employees work Monday through Friday, from 9 to 5, in the same office. The notion that everyone retires completely by age 65 should also be jettisoned. Companies instead should invest in opportunities for creative mentorship, part-time work, flex-hour schedules, and sabbatical programs geared to the abilities and inclinations of older workers. Programs that offer pre-retirement and career transition support, coaching, counseling, and encore career pathways can also make employees more engaged and productive. Many older workers say they are ready to exchange high salaries for flexible schedules and phased retirements. Some companies have already embraced nontraditional work programs for employees, creating a new kind of environment for success. The CVS "Snowbird" program, for example, allows older employees to travel and work seasonally in different CVS pharmacy regions. Home Depot recruits and hires thousands of retired construction workers, making the most of their expertise on the sales floor. The National Institutes of Health, half of whose workforce is over 50, actively recruits at 50-plus job fairs and offers benefits such as flexible schedules, telecommuting, and exercise classes. Steelcase offers workers a phased retirement program with reduced hours. Michelin has rehired retirees to oversee projects, foster community relations, and facilitate employee mentoring. Brooks Brothers consults with older workers on equipment and process design, and restructures assignments to offer enhanced flexibility for its aging workforce.

Reimagine the workplace

Your company should also be prepared to adjust workspaces to improve ergonomics and make environments more age-friendly for older employees. No one should be distracted from their tasks by pain that can be prevented or eased, and even small changes can improve health, safety, and productivity. Xerox, for example, has an ergonomic training program aimed at reducing musculoskeletal disorders in its aging workforce. BMW and Nissan have implemented changes to their manufacturing lines to accommodate older workers, ranging from barbershop-style chairs and better-designed tools to "cobot" (collaborative robot) partners that manage complicated tasks and lift heavier objects. The good news is that programs that improve the lives of older workers can be equally valuable for younger counterparts.

Mind the mix

Lastly, you need to consider and monitor the age mixes in your departments and teams. Many companies will need to manage as many as five generations of workers in the near future, if they aren't already. Some pernicious biases can make this difficult. For example, research shows that every generation wants meaningful work—but that each believes everyone else is just in it for the money. Companies should emphasize workers' shared value. "Companies pursuing Millennial-specific employee engagement strategies are wasting time, focus, and money," Bruce Pfau, the former vice chair of human resources at KPMG, argues. "They would be far better served to focus on factors that lead all employees to join, stay, and perform at their best."

By tapping ways that workers of different generations can augment and learn from each other, companies set themselves up for success over the long-term. Young workers can benefit from the mentorship of older colleagues, and a promising workforce resource lies in intergenerational collaboration, combining the energy and speed of youth with the wisdom and experience of age.

PNC Financial Group uses multigenerational teams to help the company compete more effectively in the financial markets through a better understanding of the target audience for products. Pharma giant Pfizer has experimented with a "senior intern" program to reap the benefits of multigenerational collaboration. In the tech world, Airbnb recruited former hotel mogul Chip Conley to provide experienced management perspective to his younger colleagues. Pairing younger and older workers in all phases of product and service innovation and design can create opportunity for professional growth. And facilitating intergenerational relationships, mentoring, training, and teaming mitigate isolation and help break down walls.

To begin this process, start talking to your employees of all ages. And get them to talk with each other about their goals, interests, needs, and worries. Young and old workers share similar anxieties and hopes about work—and also have differences that need to be better understood companywide. Look for opportunities for engagement between generations and places where older and younger workers can support one another through skill development and mentorship. After all, if everyone needs and wants to work, we're going to have to learn to work together.

To be clear, all of these changes—from flexible hours to team makeup—will require a recalibration of company processes, some of which are deeply ingrained. Leaders must ask, do our current health insurance, sick leave, caregiving, and vacation policies accommodate people who work reduced hours? Do our employee performance-measurement systems appropriately recognize and reward the strengths of older workers? Currently, most companies focus on individual achievement as opposed to team success. This may inadvertently punish older employees who offer other types of value—like mentorship, forging deep relationships with clients and colleagues, and conflict resolution—that are not as easily captured using traditional assessment tools. Here, too, initiatives aimed at older workers can benefit other workers as well. For instance, research suggests that evaluating team performance also tends to boost the careers of employees from low-income backgrounds.

Turning a Crisis into an Opportunity

I'm admittedly bullish about the positive aspects of working longer and believe that company leaders can harness the opportunity of an aging population to gain competitive advantage. But I'm not oblivious to the challenges a longevity strategy poses. We're talking about initiating a massive culture change for firms—a change that must come from the top.

But ignoring the realities of the demographic shift under way is no longer an option. CEOs and senior executives will need to put the issue front and center with HR leaders, product developers, marketing managers, investors, and many other stakeholders who may not have it on their radar screens. This will take guts and persistence: Leaders must bravely say, "We reject the assumption that people become less tech-savvy as they get older" and "We will fight the impulse to put only our youngest employees on new initiatives." To genuinely make headway on this long-range issue, companies will have to make tough, and sometimes unpopular, decisions, especially in a world where short-term results and demands dominate leaders' agendas. But isn't that what great leaders do?

The business community has a chance to spearhead a broad movement to change culture, create opportunity, and drive growth. In doing so, companies will improve not only mature lives, but lives of all ages, and the prospects of workers for generations to come. This transformative movement to realize the potential of the 21st century's changing demography is the next big test for corporate leadership.

Originally published on hbr.org in November 2018. Reprint BG1806

Neurodiversity as a Competitive Advantage

by Robert D. Austin and Gary P. Pisano

MEET JOHN. HE'S A WIZARD at data analytics. His combination of mathematical ability and software development skill is highly unusual. His CV features two master's degrees, both with honors. An obvious guy for a tech company to scoop up, right?

Until recently, no. Before John ran across a firm that had begun experimenting with alternative approaches to talent, he was unemployed for more than two years. Other companies he had talked with badly needed the skills he possessed. But he couldn't make it through the hiring process.

If you watched John for a while, you'd start to see why. He seems, well, different. He wears headphones all the time, and when people talk to him, he doesn't look right at them. He leans over every 10 minutes or so to tighten his shoelaces; he can't concentrate when they're loose. When they're tight, though, John is the department's most productive employee. He is hardworking and never wants to take breaks. Although his assigned workplace "buddy" has finally persuaded him to do so, he doesn't enjoy them.

"John" is a composite of people whose privacy we wanted to protect—people with autism spectrum disorder. He is representative of participants in the programs of pioneering companies that have begun seeking out "neurodiverse" talent.

A lot of people are like John. The incidence of autism in the United States is now 1 in 42 among boys and 1 in 189 among girls, according to the Centers for Disease Control and Prevention. And although corporate programs have so far focused primarily on autistic people, it should be possible to extend them to people affected by dyspraxia (a neurologically based physical disorder), dyslexia, ADHD, social anxiety disorders, and other conditions. Many people with these disorders have higher-than-average abilities; research shows that some conditions, including autism and dyslexia, can bestow special skills in pattern recognition, memory, or mathematics. Yet those affected often struggle to fit the profiles sought by prospective employers.

Neurodiverse people frequently need workplace accommodations, such as headphones to prevent auditory overstimulation, to activate or maximally leverage their abilities. Sometimes they exhibit challenging eccentricities. In many cases the accommodations and challenges are manageable and the potential returns are great. But to realize the benefits, most companies would have to adjust their recruitment, selection, and career development policies to reflect a broader definition of talent.

A growing number of prominent companies have reformed their HR processes in order to access neurodiverse talent; among them are SAP, Hewlett Packard Enterprise (HPE), Microsoft, Willis Towers Watson, Ford, and EY. Many others, including Caterpillar, Dell Technologies, Deloitte, IBM, JPMorgan Chase, and UBS, have start-up or exploratory efforts under way. We have had extensive access to the neurodiversity programs at SAP, HPE, and Specialisterne (the Danish consulting company that originated such programs) and have also interacted with people at Microsoft, Willis Towers Watson, and EY.

Although the programs are still in early days—SAP's, the longest running among major companies, is just four years old—managers say they are already paying off in ways far beyond reputational enhancement. Those ways include productivity gains, quality improvement, boosts in innovative capabilities, and broad increases in employee engagement. Nick Wilson, the managing director of HPE South Pacific—an organization with

Idea in Brief

The Problem

Many people with neurological conditions such as autism spectrum disorder, dyspraxia, and dyslexia have extraordinary skills, including in pattern recognition, memory, and mathematics. But the neurodiverse population remains largely untapped.

The Cause

Conventional recruitment and career-development methods (for example, job interviews) and the belief that scalable work processes require absolute conformity to standardized approaches screen out neurodiverse people who could be valuable employees.

The Solution

A growing number of companies—among them SAP, Hewlett Packard Enterprise, Microsoft, Willis Towers Watson, and EY—have reformed HR practices to capitalize on the talents of neurodiverse people. In the process, they are becoming better able to fully leverage the skills of *all* workers.

one of the largest such programs—says that no other initiative in his company delivers benefits at so many levels.

Perhaps the most surprising benefit is that managers have begun thinking more deeply about leveraging the talents of *all* employees through greater sensitivity to individual needs. SAP's program "forces you to get to know the person better, so you know how to manage them," says Silvio Bessa, the senior vice president of digital business services. "It's made me a better manager, without a doubt."

Why Neurodiversity Presents Opportunities

"Neurodiversity is the idea that neurological differences like autism and ADHD are the result of normal, natural variation in the human genome," John Elder Robison, a scholar in residence and a cochair of the Neurodiversity Working Group at the College of William & Mary, writes in a blog on *Psychology Today's* website. Robison, who himself has Asperger's syndrome, adds, "Indeed, many individuals who embrace the concept of neurodiversity believe that people with differences do not need to be cured; they need help and accommodation instead." We couldn't agree more.

Everyone is to some extent *differently abled* (an expression favored by many neurodiverse people), because we are all born different and raised differently. Our ways of thinking result from both our inherent "machinery" and the experiences that have "programmed" us.

Most managers are familiar with the advantages organizations can gain from diversity in the backgrounds, disciplinary training, gender, culture, and other individual qualities of employees. Benefits from neurodiversity are similar but more direct. Because neurodiverse people are wired differently from "neurotypical" people, they may bring new perspectives to a company's efforts to create or recognize value. At HPE, neurodiverse software testers observed that one client's projects always seemed to go into crisis mode before a launch. Intolerant of disorder, they strenuously questioned the company's apparent acceptance of the chaos. This led the client company to realize that it had indeed become too tolerant of these crises and, with the help of the testers, to successfully redesign the launch process. At SAP, a neurodiverse customer-support analyst spotted an opportunity to let customers help solve a common problem themselves; thousands of them subsequently used the resources he created.

Nevertheless, the neurodiverse population remains a largely untapped talent pool. Unemployment runs as high as 80% (this figure includes people with more-severe disorders, who are not candidates for neurodiversity programs). When they are working, even highly capable neurodiverse people are often underemployed. Program participants told us story after story of how, despite having solid credentials, they had previously had to settle for the kinds of jobs many people leave behind in high school. When SAP began its Autism at Work program, applicants included people with master's degrees in electrical engineering, biostatistics, economic statistics, and anthropology and bachelor's degrees in computer science, applied and computational mathematics, electrical engineering, and engineering physics. Some had dual degrees. Many had earned very high grades and graduated with honors or other distinctions. One held a patent.

Not surprisingly, when autistic people with those sorts of credentials do manage to get hired, many turn out to be capable, and some are really great. Over the past two years HPE's program has placed more than 30 participants in software-testing roles at Australia's Department of Human Services (DHS). Preliminary results suggest that the organization's neurodiverse testing teams are 30% more productive than the others.

Inspired by the successes at DHS, the Australian Defense Department is now working with HPE to develop a neurodiversity program in cybersecurity; participants will apply their superior pattern-detection abilities to tasks such as examining logs and other sources of messy data for signs of intrusion or attack. Using assessment methods borrowed from the Israeli Defense Forces (IDF), it has found candidates whose relevant abilities are "off the charts." (The IDF's Special Intelligence Unit 9900, which is responsible for analyzing aerial and satellite imagery, has a group staffed primarily with people on the autism spectrum. It has proved that they can spot patterns others do not see.)

The case for neurodiverse hiring is especially compelling given the skills shortages that increasingly afflict technology and other industries. For example, the European Union faces a shortage of 800,000 IT workers by 2020, according to a European Commission study. The biggest deficits are expected to be in strategically important and rapidly expanding areas such as data analytics and IT services implementation, whose tasks are a good match with the abilities of some neurodiverse people.

Why Companies Don't Tap Neurodiverse Talent

What has kept so many companies from taking on people with the skills they badly need? It comes down to the way they find and recruit talent and decide whom to hire (and promote).

Especially in large companies, HR processes are developed with an eye toward wide application across the organization. But there is a conflict between scalability and the goal of acquiring neurodiverse talent. "SAP focuses on having scalable HR processes; however, if we were to use the same processes for everyone, we would miss people with autism," says Anka Wittenberg, the company's chief diversity and inclusion officer.

In addition, the behaviors of many neurodiverse people run counter to common notions of what makes a good employee—solid communication skills, being a team player, emotional intelligence, persuasiveness, salesperson-type personalities, the ability to network, the ability to conform to standard practices without special accommodations, and so on. These criteria systematically screen out neurodiverse people.

But they are not the only way to provide value. In fact, in recent decades the ability to compete on the basis of *innovation* has become more crucial for many companies. Innovation calls on firms to add variety to the mix—to include people and ideas from "the edges," as SAP put it in the press release announcing its program. Having people who see things differently and who maybe don't fit in seamlessly "helps offset our tendency, as a big company, to all look in the same direction," Bessa says.

You might think that organizations could simply seek more variety in prospective employees while retaining their traditional recruiting, hiring, and development practices. Many have taken that approach: Their managers still work top down from strategies to capabilities needed, translating those into organizational roles, job descriptions, and recruiting checklists. But two big problems cause them to miss neurodiverse talent.

The first involves a practice that is almost universal under the traditional approach: interviewing. Although neurodiverse people may excel in important areas, many don't interview well. For example, autistic people often don't make good eye contact, are prone to conversational tangents, and can be overly honest about their weaknesses. Some have confidence problems arising from difficulties they experienced in previous interview situations. Neurodiverse people more broadly are unlikely to earn higher scores in interviews than less-talented neurotypical candidates. SAP and HPE have found that it can take weeks or months to discover how good some program participants are (or, equally important, where their limitations lie). Fortunately, as we'll see, interviews are not the only way to assess a candidate's suitability.

The second problem, especially common in large companies, derives from the assumption that scalable processes require absolute conformity to standardized approaches. As mentioned, employees in neurodiversity programs typically need to be allowed to deviate from established practices. This shifts a manager's orientation from assuring compliance through standardization to adjusting individual work contexts. Most accommodations, such as installing different lighting and providing noise-canceling headphones, are not very expensive. But they do require managers to tailor individual work settings more than they otherwise might.

How Pioneers Are Changing the Talent Management Game

The tech industry has a history of hiring oddballs. The talented nerd who lacks social graces has become a cultural icon, as much a part of the industry mythos as the company that starts in a garage. In his book *NeuroTribes,* Steve Silberman points out that the incidence of autism is particularly high in places like Silicon Valley (for reasons not completely understood). He and others have hypothesized that many of the industry's "oddballs" and "nerds" might well have been "on the spectrum," although undiagnosed. Hiring for neurodiversity, then, could be seen as an extension of the tendencies of a culture that recognizes the value of nerds.

In recent years a few pioneering companies have formalized and professionalized those tendencies. Although their programs vary, they have elements in common, not least because they draw on the body of knowledge developed at Specialisterne. Thorkil Sonne founded the firm in 2004, motivated by the autism diagnosis of his third child. Over the next several years it developed and refined noninterview methods for assessing, training, and managing neurodiverse talent and demonstrated the viability of its model by running a successful for-profit company focused on software testing.

Dissatisfied with the rate at which his own company could create jobs, Sonne established the Specialist People Foundation (recently renamed the Specialisterne Foundation) in 2008 to spread his company's know-how to others and persuade multinationals to start neurodiversity programs. Most companies that have done so have worked with the foundation to deploy some version of the Specialisterne approach. It has seven major elements:

Team with "social partners" for expertise you lack

Managers in, say, a tech company know a lot about many things but usually are not experts in autism or other categories of neurodiversity. Also, for many good reasons, companies hesitate to extend their activities into employees' private lives, where neurodiverse people may need extra help.

To fill these gaps, the companies we studied entered into relationships with "social partners"—government or nonprofit organizations committed to helping people with disabilities obtain jobs. SAP has worked with California's Department of Rehabilitation, Pennsylvania's Office of Vocational Rehabilitation, the U.S. nonprofits EXPANDability and the Arc, and overseas agencies such as EnAble India, while HPE has worked with Autism SA (South Australia). Such groups help companies navigate local employment regulations that apply to people with disabilities, suggest candidates from lists of neurodiverse people seeking employment, assist in prescreening, help arrange public funding for training, sometimes administer training, and provide the mentorship and ongoing support (especially outside work hours) needed to ensure that neurodiverse employees will succeed. In Germany, recognition of the benefits of moving people off public assistance and into jobs that generate tax revenue has led to publicly funded positions to support the retention of neurodiverse employees. Although estimates of the benefits a government gains by turning such people into tax-paying tech workers vary, they often are on the order of $50,000 per person a year.

Use nontraditional, noninterview-based assessment and training processes

To this end, Specialisterne created "hangouts"—comfortable gatherings, usually lasting half a day, in which neurodiverse job candidates can demonstrate their abilities in casual interactions with company managers. At the end of a hangout, some candidates are selected for two to six weeks of further assessment and training (the duration varies by company). During this time they use Lego Mindstorms robotic construction and programming kits to work on assigned projects—first individually and then in groups, with the projects becoming more like actual work as the process continues. Some companies have additional sessions. SAP, for example, established a "soft skills" module to help candidates who have never worked in a professional environment become familiar with the norms of such a setting. These efforts are typically funded by the government or nonprofits. Trainees are usually paid.

Despite the social difficulties experienced by many neurodiverse people, candidates often display complex collaborative and support behaviors during the project-based assessment period. At HPE, for example, groups were asked to devise a reliable robotic pill-dispensing system. During the presentation of solutions, one candidate froze. "I'm sorry, I can't do it," he said. "The words are all jumbled up in my head." His neurodiverse teammates rushed to his rescue, surrounding and reassuring him, and he was able to finish.

By extending the assessment process, such programs allow time for candidates' capabilities to surface. There are, of course, other ways to do this. HPE has begun using internships that include similar elements.

Train other workers and managers

Short (some are just half a day), low-key training sessions help existing employees understand what to expect from their new colleagues—for example, that they might need accommodations and might seem different. Managers get somewhat more-extensive training to familiarize them with sources of support for program employees.

Set up a support ecosystem

Companies with neurodiverse programs design and maintain simple support systems for their new employees. SAP defines two "support circles"—one for the workplace, the other for an employee's personal life. The workplace support circle includes a team manager, a team buddy, a job and life skills coach, a work mentor, and an "HR business partner," who oversees a group of program participants. Buddies are staff members on the same team who provide assistance with daily tasks, workload management, and prioritization. Job and life skills coaches are usually from social partner organizations. Other social partner roles include vocational rehab counselor and personal counselor. Usually, families of employees also provide support.

HPE takes a different approach. It places new neurodiverse employees in "pods" of about 15 people, where they work alongside neurotypical colleagues in a roughly 4:1 ratio while two managers and a consultant are tasked with addressing neurodiversity-related issues.

Tailor methods for managing careers

Employees hired through these programs need long-term career paths, just as other workers do. This requires serious thought about ongoing assessment and development that will take the special circumstances of neurodiverse employment into account. Fortunately, over time supervisors usually get a good sense of program employees' talents and limitations. Participants undergo the same performance evaluations that other employees do, but managers work within those processes to set specific goals. Although some goals may relate to participants' conditions, no allowances are made for unsatisfactory performance. If anything, neurodiverse employees must satisfy *more* requirements than others, because they must meet program objectives in addition to the performance objectives expected of anyone in their role.

Some participants quickly demonstrate potential to become integrated into the mainstream organization and go further in their careers. HPE's pods are designed to provide a safe environment in which participants can build skills that will allow them to perform well and eventually to transition out of their pods into more-mainstream jobs.

Scale the program

SAP has announced an intention to make 1% of its workforce neurodiverse by 2020—a number chosen because it roughly corresponds to the percentage of autistic people in the general population.

Microsoft, HPE, and others are also working to enlarge their programs, although they have declined to set numerical targets. It's easiest to expand employment in those areas, such as software testing, business analytics, and cybersecurity, in which tasks are a good fit with neurodiverse talent. SAP, however, has placed its more than 100 program employees in 18 roles. "The original expectation, as I understood it, was that these colleagues would be mostly focused on repetitive work, such as software testing," one manager told us. "But in practice they have been able to add value in a much broader range of tasks." Those include product management, which involves coordinating the development of new SAP offerings; HR service associate, which entails organizing and planning HR activities; associate consultant, which requires helping customers apply SAP solutions to business problems; and customer support, which means working with customers on the phone to help them use SAP software. The latter two defy the assumption that people with autism can't hold jobs that require social skills.

HPE is deploying neurodiverse specialists nine at a time, in pods, to client organizations—in effect, selling packages of the advanced capabilities derived from neurodiversity. The model has intriguing scale possibilities, both because many workers are placed at once and because client demand enlarges the domain of possible placements.

Mainstream the program

The success of neurodiversity programs has prompted some companies to think about how ordinary HR processes may be excluding high-quality talent. SAP is conducting a review to determine how recruiting, hiring, and development could take a broader view. Its stated goal is to make its mainstream talent processes so "neurodiversity friendly" that it can ultimately close its neurodiversity program. Microsoft has similar ambitions.

Companies have experienced a surprising array of benefits from neurodiversity programs. Some are straightforward: Firms have become more successful at finding and hiring good and even great talent in tough-to-fill skills categories. Products, services, and bottom lines have profited from lower defect rates and higher productivity. Both SAP and HPE report examples of neurodiverse employees' participating on teams that generated significant innovations (one, at SAP, helped develop a technical fix worth an estimated $40 million in savings).

Other benefits are subtler. One executive told us that efforts to make corporate communications more direct, in order to account for the difficulties autistic employees have with nuance, irony, and other fine points of language, have improved communication overall. The perfectionist tendencies of some HPE software-testing pods have caused client organizations to raise their game and stop viewing certain common problems as inevitable. In addition, employee engagement has risen in areas the programs touch: Neurotypical people report that involvement makes their work more meaningful and their morale higher. And early indications suggest that program employees, appreciative of having been given a chance, are very loyal and have low rates of turnover.

Last but not least, the programs confer reputational benefits. The companies that pioneered them have been recognized by the United Nations as exemplars of responsible management and have won global corporate citizenship awards.

Challenges of a Neurodiverse Workforce

To be sure, companies implementing neurodiversity programs have encountered challenges. Although there are plenty of potential candidates, many are hard to identify, because universities—sensitive to issues of discrimination—do not classify students in neurodiversity terms, and potential candidates do not necessarily self-identify. In response, HPE is helping colleges and high schools set up nontraditional "work experience" programs for neurodiverse populations. These involve video gaming, robotic programming, and other activities. Microsoft, too, is working with universities to improve methods of identifying and accessing neurodiverse talent.

Another common difficulty involves the dashed hopes of candidates who are not chosen for placement—an inevitable circumstance that must be handled carefully. At one company, parents whose son did not qualify for a job wrote to the CEO; the program had raised their hopes that he would finally achieve meaningful employment, and they were understandably disappointed. Executives fretted about a potential PR problem. In the end, compassionate discussions between the parents and managers of the program—some of whom had families that had experienced similar issues—calmed the situation.

Issues related to fairness and norms of interaction might arise as well. In one case we encountered, a program participant who had overstimulation difficulties was given his own office while four people in a nearby department were crowded into a similar space, generating complaints. Those subsided after an explanation was offered. We also heard of instances in which the excessive honesty typical of autistic people raised hackles. One concerned a program employee who told a colleague, "You stink at your job." Coaching by managers and mentors can help address such situations.

Some supervisors reported that the program generated extra work for them. For instance, the perfectionist tendencies of some participants made it difficult for those employees to judge which defects were worth fixing, which were not, and which required them to seek additional direction.

Managing neurodiverse employees' stress presents another challenge. We heard reports that unexpected and uncontrollable events, such as systems outages that interfered with work routines, caused unusually high levels of anxiety among participants. Many people we interviewed emphasized the need to be sensitive to program employees' stress. To keep it under control, some participants work only part-time—a limitation that may create problems, especially when deadlines loom.

To handle such situations, organizations need people in place who can spot and address issues before they escalate. Many managers said that with these and other supports, they could perform their jobs in a fairly normal fashion. And contrary to their initial assumptions, SAP managers found they could even supervise program participants remotely, as long as buddies and mentors provided support locally.

A Major Shift in Managing People

Neurodiversity programs induce companies and their leaders to adopt a style of management that emphasizes placing each person in a context that maximizes her or his contributions.

SAP uses a metaphor to communicate this idea across the organization: People are like puzzle pieces, irregularly shaped. Historically, companies have asked employees to trim away their irregularities, because it's easier to fit people together if they are all perfect rectangles. But that requires employees to leave their differences at home—differences firms need in order to innovate. "The corporate world has mostly missed out on this [benefit]," Anka Wittenberg observes.

This suggests that companies must embrace an alternative philosophy, one that calls on managers to do the hard work of fitting irregular puzzle pieces together—to treat people not as containers of fungible human resources but as unique individual assets. The work for managers will be harder. But the payoff for companies will be considerable: access to more of their employees' talents along with diverse perspectives that may help them compete more effectively. "Innovation," Wittenberg notes, "is most likely to come from parts of us that we don't all share."

Originally published in May–June 2017. Reprint R1703F

Managing
Multicultural Teams

by Jeanne Brett, Kristin Behfar, and Mary C. Kern

WHEN A MAJOR INTERNATIONAL SOFTWARE developer needed to produce a new product quickly, the project manager assembled a team of employees from India and the United States. From the start the team members could not agree on a delivery date for the product. The Americans thought the work could be done in two to three weeks; the Indians predicted it would take two to three months. As time went on, the Indian team members proved reluctant to report setbacks in the production process, which the American team members would find out about only when work was due to be passed to them. Such conflicts, of course, may affect any team, but in this case they arose from cultural differences. As tensions mounted, conflict over delivery dates and feedback became personal, disrupting team members' communication about even mundane issues. The project manager decided he had to intervene—with the result that both the American and the Indian team members came to rely on him for direction regarding minute operational details that the team should have been able to handle itself. The manager became so bogged down by quotidian issues that the project careened hopelessly off even the most pessimistic schedule—and the team never learned to work together effectively.

Multicultural teams often generate frustrating management dilemmas. Cultural differences can create substantial obstacles to effective teamwork—but these may be subtle and difficult to recognize until significant damage has already been done. As in the case above, which the manager involved told us about, managers may create more problems than they resolve by intervening. The challenge in managing multicultural teams effectively is to recognize underlying cultural causes of conflict, and to intervene in ways that both get the team back on track and empower its members to deal with future challenges themselves.

We interviewed managers and members of multicultural teams from all over the world. These interviews, combined with our deep research on dispute resolution and teamwork, led us to conclude that the wrong kind of managerial intervention may sideline valuable members who should be participating or, worse, create resistance, resulting in poor team performance. We're not talking here about respecting differing national standards for doing business, such as accounting practices. We're referring to day-to-day working problems among team members that can keep multicultural teams from realizing the very gains they were set up to harvest, such as knowledge of different product markets, culturally sensitive customer service, and 24-hour work rotations.

The good news is that cultural challenges are manageable if managers and team members choose the right strategy and avoid imposing single-culture-based approaches on multicultural situations.

The Challenges

People tend to assume that challenges on multicultural teams arise from differing styles of communication. But this is only one of the four categories that, according to our research, can create barriers to a team's ultimate success. These categories are direct versus indirect communication; trouble with accents and fluency; differing attitudes toward hierarchy and authority; and conflicting norms for decision making.

Direct versus indirect communication
Communication in Western cultures is typically direct and explicit. The meaning is on the surface, and a listener doesn't have to know

Idea in Brief

If your company does business internationally, you're probably leading teams with members from diverse cultural backgrounds. Those differences can present serious obstacles. For example, some members' lack of fluency in the team's dominant language can lead others to underestimate their competence. When such obstacles arise, your team can stalemate.

To get the team moving again, avoid intervening directly, advise Brett, Behfar, and Kern. Though sometimes necessary, your involvement can prevent team members from solving problems themselves—and learning from that process.

Instead, choose one of three indirect interventions. When possible, encourage team members to **adapt** by acknowledging cultural gaps and working around them. If your team isn't able to be open about their differences, consider **structural intervention** (e.g., reassigning members to reduce interpersonal friction). As a last resort, use an **exit** strategy (e.g., removing a member from the team).

There's no one right way to tackle multicultural problems. But understanding four barriers to team success can help you begin evaluating possible responses.

much about the context or the speaker to interpret it. This is not true in many other cultures, where meaning is embedded in the way the message is presented. For example, Western negotiators get crucial information about the other party's preferences and priorities by asking direct questions, such as "Do you prefer option A or option B?" In cultures that use indirect communication, negotiators may have to infer preferences and priorities from changes—or the lack of them—in the other party's settlement proposal. In cross-cultural negotiations, the non-Westerner can understand the direct communications of the Westerner, but the Westerner has difficulty understanding the indirect communications of the non-Westerner.

An American manager who was leading a project to build an interface for a U.S. and Japanese customer-data system explained the problems her team was having this way: "In Japan, they want to talk and discuss. Then we take a break and they talk within the organization. They want to make sure that there's harmony in the rest of the organization. One of the hardest lessons for me was when I thought they were saying yes but they just meant 'I'm listening to you.'"

Idea in Practice

Four Barriers

The following cultural differences can cause destructive conflicts in a team:

- **Direct versus indirect communication.** Some team members use direct, explicit communication while others are indirect, for example, asking questions instead of pointing out problems with a project. When members see such differences as violations of their culture's communication norms, relationships can suffer.

- **Trouble with accents and fluency.** Members who aren't fluent in the team's dominant language may have difficulty communicating their knowledge. This can prevent the team from using their expertise and create frustration or perceptions of incompetence.

- **Differing attitudes toward hierarchy.** Team members from hierarchical cultures expect to be treated differently according to their status in the organization. Members from egalitarian cultures do not. Failure of some members to honor those expectations can cause humiliation or loss of stature and credibility.

- **Conflicting decision-making norms.** Members vary in how quickly they make decisions and in how much analysis they require beforehand. Someone who prefers making decisions quickly may grow frustrated with those who need more time.

Four Interventions

Your team's unique circumstances can help you determine how to respond to multicultural conflicts. Consider these options:

Intervention type	When to use	Example
Adaptation: working with or around differences	Members are willing to acknowledge cultural differences and figure out how to live with them.	An American engineer working on a team that included Israelis was shocked by their in-your-face, argumentative style. Once he noticed they confronted each other and not just him—and still worked well together—he realized confrontations weren't personal attacks and accepted their style.

Intervention type	When to use	Example
Structural intervention: reorganizing to reduce friction	The team has obvious subgroups, or members cling to negative stereotypes of one another.	An international research team's leader realized that when he led meetings, members "shut down" because they felt intimidated by his executive status. After he hired a consultant to run future meetings, members participated more.
Managerial intervention: making final decisions without team involvement	Rarely; for instance, a new team needs guidance in establishing productive norms.	A software development team's lingua franca was English, but some members spoke with pronounced accents. The manager explained they'd been chosen for their task expertise, not fluency in English. And she directed them to tell customers: "I realize I have an accent. If you don't understand what I'm saying, just stop me and ask questions."
Exit: voluntary or involuntary removal of a team member	Emotions are running high, and too much face has been lost on both sides to salvage the situation.	When two members of a multicultural consulting team couldn't resolve their disagreement over how to approach problems, one member left the firm.

The differences between direct and indirect communication can cause serious damage to relationships when team projects run into problems. When the American manager quoted above discovered that several flaws in the system would significantly disrupt company operations, she pointed this out in an e-mail to her American boss and the Japanese team members. Her boss appreciated the direct warnings; her Japanese colleagues were embarrassed, because she had violated their norms for uncovering and discussing problems. Their reaction was to provide her with less access to the people and information she needed to monitor progress. They would probably have responded better if she had pointed out the problems indirectly—for example, by asking them what would happen if a certain part of the system was not functioning properly, even though she knew full well that it was malfunctioning and also what the implications were.

As our research indicates is so often true, communication challenges create barriers to effective teamwork by reducing information sharing, creating interpersonal conflict, or both. In Japan, a typical response to direct confrontation is to isolate the norm violator. This American manager was isolated not just socially but also physically. She told us, "They literally put my office in a storage room, where I had desks stacked from floor to ceiling and I was the only person there. So they totally isolated me, which was a pretty loud signal to me that I was not a part of the inside circle and that they would communicate with me only as needed."

Her direct approach had been intended to solve a problem, and in one sense, it did, because her project was launched problem-free. But her norm violations exacerbated the challenges of working with her Japanese colleagues and limited her ability to uncover any other problems that might have derailed the project later on.

Trouble with accents and fluency
Although the language of international business is English, misunderstandings or deep frustration may occur because of nonnative speakers' accents, lack of fluency, or problems with translation or usage. These may also influence perceptions of status or competence.

For example, a Latin American member of a multicultural consulting team lamented, "Many times I felt that because of the language difference, I didn't have the words to say some things that I was thinking. I noticed that when I went to these interviews with the U.S. guy, he would tend to lead the interviews, which was understandable but also disappointing, because we are at the same level. I had very good questions, but he would take the lead."

When we interviewed an American member of a U.S.-Japanese team that was assessing the potential expansion of a U.S. retail chain into Japan, she described one American teammate this way: "He was not interested in the Japanese consultants' feedback and felt that because they weren't as fluent as he was, they weren't intelligent enough and, therefore, could add no value." The team member described was responsible for assessing one aspect of the feasibility of expansion into Japan. Without input from the Japanese experts, he risked overestimating opportunities and underestimating challenges.

Nonfluent team members may well be the most expert on the team, but their difficulty communicating knowledge makes it hard for the team to recognize and utilize their expertise. If teammates become frustrated or impatient with a lack of fluency, interpersonal conflicts can arise. Nonnative speakers may become less motivated to contribute, or anxious about their performance evaluations and future career prospects. The organization as a whole pays a greater price: Its investment in a multicultural team fails to pay off.

Some teams, we learned, use language differences to resolve (rather than create) tensions. A team of U.S. and Latin American buyers was negotiating with a team from a Korean supplier. The negotiations took place in Korea, but the discussions were conducted in English. Frequently the Koreans would caucus at the table by speaking Korean. The buyers, frustrated, would respond by appearing to caucus in Spanish—though they discussed only inconsequential current events and sports, in case any of the Koreans spoke Spanish. Members of the team who didn't speak Spanish pretended to participate, to the great amusement of their teammates. This approach proved effective: It conveyed to the Koreans in an appropriately indirect way that their caucuses in Korean were frustrating and annoying to the other side. As a result, both teams cut back on sidebar conversations.

Differing attitudes toward hierarchy and authority

A challenge inherent in multicultural teamwork is that by design, teams have a rather flat structure. But team members from some cultures, in which people are treated differently according to their status in an organization, are uncomfortable on flat teams. If they defer to higher-status team members, their behavior will be seen as appropriate when most of the team comes from a hierarchical culture; but they may damage their stature and credibility—and even face humiliation—if most of the team comes from an egalitarian culture.

One manager of Mexican heritage, who was working on a credit and underwriting team for a bank, told us, "In Mexican culture, you're always supposed to be humble. So whether you understand something or not, you're supposed to put it in the form of a question. You have to keep it open-ended, out of respect. I think that actually worked against me, because the Americans thought I really didn't know what I was talking about. So it made me feel like they thought I was wavering on my answer."

When, as a result of differing cultural norms, team members believe they've been treated disrespectfully, the whole project can blow up. In another Korean-U.S. negotiation, the American members of a due diligence team were having difficulty getting information from their Korean counterparts, so they complained directly to higher-level Korean management, nearly wrecking the deal. The higher-level managers were offended because hierarchy is strictly adhered to in Korean organizations and culture. It should have been their own lower-level people, not the U.S. team members, who came to them with a problem. And the Korean team members were mortified that their bosses had been involved before they themselves could brief them. The crisis was resolved only when high-level U.S. managers made a trip to Korea, conveying appropriate respect for their Korean counterparts.

Conflicting norms for decision making

Cultures differ enormously when it comes to decision making—particularly, how quickly decisions should be made and how much analysis is required beforehand. Not surprisingly, U.S. managers like to make decisions very quickly and with relatively little analysis by comparison with managers from other countries.

A Brazilian manager at an American company who was negotiating to buy Korean products destined for Latin America told us, "On the first day, we agreed on three points, and on the second day, the U.S.-Spanish side wanted to start with point four. But the Korean side wanted to go back and rediscuss points one through three. My boss almost had an attack."

What U.S. team members learn from an experience like this is that the American way simply cannot be imposed on other cultures. Managers from other cultures may, for example, decline to share information until they understand the full scope of a project. But they have learned that they can't simply ignore the desire of their American counterparts to make decisions quickly. What to do? The best solution seems to be to make minor concessions on process— to learn to adjust to and even respect another approach to decision making. For example, American managers have learned to keep their impatient bosses away from team meetings and give them frequent if brief updates. A comparable lesson for managers from other cultures is to be explicit about what they need—saying, for example, "We have to see the big picture before we talk details."

Four Strategies

The most successful teams and managers we interviewed used four strategies for dealing with these challenges: adaptation (acknowledging cultural gaps openly and working around them), structural intervention (changing the shape of the team), managerial intervention (setting norms early or bringing in a higher-level manager), and exit (removing a team member when other options have failed). There is no one right way to deal with a particular kind of multicultural problem; identifying the type of challenge is only the first step. The more crucial step is assessing the circumstances—or "enabling situational conditions"—under which the team is working. For example, does the project allow any flexibility for change, or do deadlines make that impossible? Are there additional resources available that might be tapped? Is the team permanent or temporary? Does the team's manager have the autonomy to make a decision about changing the team in some way? Once the situational conditions have been analyzed, the team's leader can identify an appropriate response (see the table "Identifying the right strategy").

Identifying the right strategy

The most successful teams and managers we interviewed use four strategies for dealing with problems: adaptation (acknowledging cultural gaps openly and working around them), structural intervention (changing the shape of the team), managerial intervention (setting norms early or bringing in a higher-level manager), and exit (removing a team member when other options have failed). Adaptation is the ideal strategy because the team works effectively to solve its own problem with minimal input from management—and, most important, learns from the experience. The guide below can help you identify the right strategy once you have identified both the problem and the "enabling situational conditions" that apply to the team.

Representative problems	Enabling situational conditions	Strategy	Complicating factors
• Conflict arises from decision-making differences • Misunderstanding or stonewalling arises from communication differences	• Team members can attribute a challenge to culture rather than personality • Higher-level managers are not available or the team would be embarrassed to involve them	**Adaptation**	• Team members must be exceptionally aware • Negotiating a common understanding takes time
• The team is affected by emotional tensions relating to fluency issues or prejudice • Team members are inhibited by perceived status differences among teammates	• The team can be subdivided to mix cultures or expertise • Tasks can be subdivided	**Structural intervention**	• If team members aren't carefully distributed, subgroups can strengthen pre-existing differences • Subgroup solutions have to fit back together

Representative problems	Enabling situational conditions	Strategy	Complicating factors
• Violations of hierarchy have resulted in loss of face • An absence of ground rules is causing conflict	• The problem has produced a high level of emotion • The team has reached a stalemate • A higher-level manager is able and willing to intervene	**Managerial intervention**	• The team becomes overly dependent on the manager • Team members may be sidelined or resistant
• A team member cannot adjust to the challenge at hand and has become unable to contribute to the project	• The team is permanent rather than temporary • Emotions are beyond the point of intervention • Too much face has been lost	**Exit**	• Talent and training costs are lost

Adaptation

Some teams find ways to work with or around the challenges they face, adapting practices or attitudes without making changes to the group's membership or assignments. Adaptation works when team members are willing to acknowledge and name their cultural differences and to assume responsibility for figuring out how to live with them. It's often the best possible approach to a problem, because it typically involves less managerial time than other strategies; and because team members participate in solving the problem themselves, they learn from the process. When team members have this mind-set, they can be creative about protecting their own substantive differences while acceding to the processes of others.

An American software engineer located in Ireland who was working with an Israeli account management team from his own company told us how shocked he was by the Israelis' in-your-face style: "There were definitely different ways of approaching issues and discussing them. There is something pretty common to the Israeli culture: They like to argue. I tend to try to collaborate more, and it got very stressful for me until I figured out how to kind of merge the cultures."

The software engineer adapted. He imposed some structure on the Israelis that helped him maintain his own style of being thoroughly prepared; that accommodation enabled him to accept the Israeli style. He also noticed that team members weren't just confronting him; they confronted one another but were able to work together effectively nevertheless. He realized that the confrontation was not personal but cultural.

In another example, an American member of a postmerger consulting team was frustrated by the hierarchy of the French company his team was working with. He felt that a meeting with certain French managers who were not directly involved in the merger "wouldn't deliver any value to me or for purposes of the project," but said that he had come to understand that "it was very important to really involve all the people there" if the integration was ultimately to work.

A U.S. and UK multicultural team tried to use their differing approaches to decision making to reach a higher-quality decision. This approach, called fusion, is getting serious attention from political scientists and from government officials dealing with multicultural populations that want to protect their cultures rather than integrate or assimilate. If the team had relied exclusively on the Americans' "forge ahead" approach, it might not have recognized the pitfalls that lay ahead and might later have had to back up and start over. Meanwhile, the UK members would have been gritting their teeth and saying "We told you things were moving too fast." If the team had used the "Let's think about this" UK approach, it might have wasted a lot of time trying to identify every pitfall, including the most unlikely, while the U.S. members chomped at the bit and muttered about analysis paralysis. The strength of this team was that some of its members were willing to forge ahead and some were willing to work through pitfalls. To accommodate them all, the team did both—moving not quite as fast as the U.S. members would have on their own and not quite as thoroughly as the UK members would have.

Structural intervention

A structural intervention is a deliberate reorganization or reassignment designed to reduce interpersonal friction or to remove a source of conflict for one or more groups. This approach can be extremely effective when obvious subgroups demarcate the team (for example, headquarters versus national subsidiaries) or if team members are proud, defensive, threatened, or clinging to negative stereotypes of one another.

A member of an investment research team scattered across continental Europe, the UK, and the U.S. described for us how his manager resolved conflicts stemming from status differences and language tensions among the team's three "tribes." The manager started by having the team meet face-to-face twice a year, not to discuss mundane day-to-day problems (of which there were many) but to identify a set of values that the team would use to direct and evaluate its progress. At the first meeting, he realized that when he started to speak, everyone else "shut down," waiting to hear what he had to say. So he hired a consultant to run future meetings. The consultant didn't represent a hierarchical threat and was therefore able to get lots of participation from team members.

Another structural intervention might be to create smaller working groups of mixed cultures or mixed corporate identities in order to get at information that is not forthcoming from the team as a whole. The manager of the team that was evaluating retail opportunities in Japan used this approach. When she realized that the female Japanese consultants would not participate if the group got large, or if their male superior was present, she broke the team up into smaller groups to try to solve problems. She used this technique repeatedly and made a point of changing the subgroups' membership each time so that team members got to know and respect everyone else on the team.

The subgrouping technique involves risks, however. It buffers people who are not working well together or not participating in the larger group for one reason or another. Sooner or later the team will have to assemble the pieces that the subgroups have come up with, so this approach relies on another structural intervention: Someone must become a mediator in order to see that the various pieces fit together.

Managerial intervention

When a manager behaves like an arbitrator or a judge, making a final decision without team involvement, neither the manager nor the team gains much insight into why the team has stalemated. But it is possible for team members to use managerial intervention effectively to sort out problems.

When an American refinery-safety expert with significant experience throughout East Asia got stymied during a project in China, she called in her company's higher-level managers in Beijing to talk to the higher-level managers to whom the Chinese refinery's managers reported. Unlike the Western team members who breached etiquette by approaching the superiors of their Korean counterparts, the safety expert made sure to respect hierarchies in both organizations.

"Trying to resolve the issues," she told us, "the local management at the Chinese refinery would end up having conferences with our Beijing office and also with the upper management within the refinery. Eventually they understood that we weren't trying to insult them or their culture or to tell them they were bad in any way. We were trying to help. They eventually understood that there were significant fire and safety issues. But we actually had to go up some levels of management to get those resolved."

Managerial intervention to set norms early in a team's life can really help the team start out with effective processes. In one instance reported to us, a multicultural software development team's lingua franca was English, but some members, though they spoke grammatically correct English, had a very pronounced accent. In setting the ground rules for the team, the manager addressed the challenge directly, telling the members that they had been chosen for their task expertise, not their fluency in English, and that the team was going to have to work around language problems. As the project moved to the customer-services training stage, the manager advised the team members to acknowledge their accents up front.

She said they should tell customers, "I realize I have an accent. If you don't understand what I'm saying, just stop me and ask questions."

Exit

Possibly because many of the teams we studied were project based, we found that leaving the team was an infrequent strategy for managing challenges. In short-term situations, unhappy team members often just waited out the project. When teams were permanent, producing products or services, the exit of one or more members was a strategy of last resort, but it was used—either voluntarily or after a formal request from management. Exit was likely when emotions were running high and too much face had been lost on both sides to salvage the situation.

An American member of a multicultural consulting team described the conflict between two senior consultants, one a Greek woman and the other a Polish man, over how to approach problems: "The woman from Greece would say, 'Here's the way I think we should do it.' It would be something that she was in control of. The guy from Poland would say, 'I think we should actually do it this way instead.' The woman would kind of turn red in the face, upset, and say, 'I just don't think that's the right way of doing it.' It would definitely switch from just professional differences to personal differences.

"The woman from Greece ended up leaving the firm. That was a direct result of probably all the different issues going on between these people. It really just wasn't a good fit. I've found that oftentimes when you're in consulting, you have to adapt to the culture, obviously, but you have to adapt just as much to the style of whoever is leading the project."

Though multicultural teams face challenges that are not directly attributable to cultural differences, such differences underlay whatever problem needed to be addressed in many of the teams we studied. Furthermore, while serious in their own right when they have a negative effect on team functioning, cultural challenges may also unmask fundamental managerial problems. Managers who intervene early and set norms; teams and managers who structure social interaction and work to engage everyone on the team; and teams that can see problems as stemming from culture, not personality, approach challenges with good humor and creativity. Managers who have to intervene when the team has reached a stalemate may be able to get the team moving again, but they seldom empower it to help itself the next time a stalemate occurs.

When frustrated team members take some time to think through challenges and possible solutions themselves, it can make a huge difference. Take, for example, this story about a financial-services call center. The members of the call-center team were all fluent Spanish-speakers, but some were North Americans and some were Latin Americans. Team performance, measured by calls answered per hour, was lagging. One Latin American was taking twice as long with her calls as the rest of the team. She was handling callers' questions appropriately, but she was also engaging in chitchat. When her teammates confronted her for being a free rider (they resented having to make up for her low call rate), she immediately acknowledged the problem, admitting that she did not know how to end the call politely—chitchat being normal in her culture. They rallied to help her: Using their technology, they would break into any of her calls that went overtime, excusing themselves to the customer, offering to take over the call, and saying that this employee was urgently needed to help out on a different call. The team's solution worked in the short run, and the employee got better at ending her calls in the long run.

In another case, the Indian manager of a multicultural team coordinating a companywide IT project found himself frustrated when he and a teammate from Singapore met with two Japanese members of the coordinating team to try to get the Japan section to deliver its part of the project. The Japanese members seemed to be saying yes, but in the Indian manager's view, their follow-through was insufficient. He considered and rejected the idea of going up the hierarchy to the Japanese team members' boss, and decided instead to try to build consensus with the whole Japanese IT team, not just the two members on the coordinating team. He and his Singapore teammate put together an eBusiness road show, took it to Japan, invited the whole IT team to view it at a lunch meeting, and walked through success stories about other parts of the organization that had aligned with the company's larger business priorities. It was rather subtle, he told us, but it worked. The Japanese IT team wanted to be spotlighted in future eBusiness road shows. In the end, the whole team worked well together—and no higher-level manager had to get involved.

Originally published in November 2006. Reprint R0611D

7 Myths About Coming Out at Work

by Raymond Trau, Jane O'Leary, and Cathy Brown

MORE AND MORE BIG BUSINESSES are providing workplace protections for LGBTIQ+ (lesbian, gay, bisexual, transgender, intersex, and queer) people.[1] It's becoming clear that when workers can bring their authentic selves to work, they are more productive and engaged. Research shows that coming out increases job satisfaction, intention to stay, and emotional support from coworkers, whereas staying "in the closet" has costs—both for the individual and the company.

And yet, many people are still reluctant to come out at work. In our study we surveyed 1,614 LGBTIQ+ Australian workers and held focus groups with 60 participants across various industries. We found that 68% of respondents were not out to everyone at work. This number decreases to 46% in the U.S., according to a Human Rights Campaign report, and 35% in the UK, according to Stonewall, the LGBT rights organization headquartered in London.

We know that when LGBTIQ+ people work in a safe environment they are more willing to come out. But while workplace policies and practices are critical, the decision to come out at work is a complex and personal one. It involves other factors, like when, how, and whom to come out to.

Our research considers this and digs below the surface to examine the experience of LGBTIQ+ people at work. We challenge myths that are drawn from common assumptions about coming out and offer suggestions to organizations that want to help their workers feel safe being themselves.

Myth #1: Coming out at work is not a big deal—after all, it's the 21st century!

Though the LGBTIQ+ community has seen big wins in the past few years—same-sex marriage is now legal in 26 countries, and around 20 have passed some kind of legislation recognizing transgender rights—coming out is still dangerous in many areas of the world and can be deadly for trans and gender-diverse people. Even in countries that are economically developed and progressive, like Australia, homosexuality has only been decriminalized since 1997, and marriage equality was just legalized in December of last year. The LGBTIQ+ rights movement is still very much in progress, and this factors into some workplace cultures and how comfortable people may feel about coming out.

Myth #2: Coming out is similar for all LGBTIQ+ people

The LGBTIQ+ community and their workplace experiences are diverse. In Australia, there has been a gradual transformation in gay and lesbian rights over the past 40 years that has also brought greater support for and protections of gay and lesbian people at work. However, trans and gender-diverse workers have historically been overlooked. They are often less willing to come out at work due to fears of discrimination and social exclusion. Our research finds that 32% of trans and gender-diverse people fear they would lose their jobs if they came out at work, as opposed to just 6% of LGB (lesbian, gay, and bisexual) people. Not surprisingly then, 49% of trans and gender-diverse workers try hard to conceal their identity from colleagues, compared to only 13% of LGB workers.

Myth #3: LGBTIQ+ workers have complete control over whether they do or don't come out at work

For some LGBTIQ+ workers, living authentically at work remains an aspiration. While almost three-quarters of our respondents in-dicated coming out is important to them, only one-third are out to everyone at work, suggesting that not everyone who *wants* to be out *feels comfortable* being out. For others, decisions about when and how to come out are often beyond their control. Some individuals are outed against their will, while others are forced to come out because of workplace policies. One transgender respondent wrote, "Give me a choice to NOT disclose—the reason HR knows I am a trans man is because it was policy for HR to process police checks when I started at my current workplace."

In fact, research shows that transgender people going through the transition process often have to come out to coworkers, causing great anxiety and distress. For some transgender people, living authentically means keeping their gender history private, particularly if they affirmed their gender identity when they were very young. For those who transition later in life, privacy is elusive. As one participant told us, "We are out merely by existing."

Myth #4: Coming out has nothing to do with work

Our research reveals that people who are able to come out at work are happier. Compared to workers who are out to some people or no one at all, those who are completely out at work are significantly more satisfied with their jobs (29% versus 16%), enthusiastic about their jobs (40% versus 26%), and proud of their work (51% versus 38%). Other research by Alexandra Sedlovskaya (at Harvard University) and colleagues finds that having a double life—being out in private life but not at work—increases social stress and depression.

Because workplaces are where people often share their personal experiences, coming out—and feeling safe enough to do so—can be about something as simple as participating in a conversation without having to have your guard up or editing what you say. For an LGBTIQ+ person, telling a story about their weekend could be an indirect way of signaling their identity.

Heterosexual and cisgender workers typically don't face the same dilemma because they are part of a majority group when it comes to sexual orientation and gender identity. They have the privilege of being seen and identified as who they really are just by being themselves. LGBTIQ+ people often must choose to come out if they want to be seen as their true selves at work. If an LGBTIQ+ person feels that they can't come out or chooses not to, others might assume that they are a member of the majority group. One gay male respondent reported, "I am more masculine and fit a certain jock/rugby stereotype and so people assume that I am straight, and I often don't correct them."

Myth #5: Coming out at work happens just once
Coming out is actually a repetitive process. It occurs not just once, but on multiple occasions. For instance, a bisexual woman may come out to her immediate manager when she is first starting a job. But later, when she feels she's gotten to know her coworkers, other managers, or clients, she might decide to come out to them too.

Among our respondents who indicated that they openly talk about their LGBTIQ+ identity at work, only 17% said they openly talk about their identity to clients. Some are concerned that being out might jeopardize client relationships and negatively impact the company as a whole. One respondent reported, "During the marriage equality vote, my organization had a big client—we are talking about a multi-million-dollar client—who said, 'If you publicly support marriage equality, you will lose our business.'" Other respondents indicated that being out at work meant risking their lives: "[With] every new client, I'm scared that it might be my last time walking the earth as I enter their house."

Myth #6: There is only one way to come out or not come out
There is a range of ways LGBTIQ+ people can signal their identities—or hide them. For instance, 47% of our respondents said they display objects like photographs, magazines, or symbols to reveal their identity at work. In contrast, 21% of our respondents said they avoid revealing their identity by keeping quiet when coworkers talk about their romantic lives, and 23% said they avoid behaving in ways that may conform to stereotypes associated with their identity group. Others who conform to heterosexual or cisgender stereotypes say they can "fly under the radar" altogether.

Myth #7: People are scared to come out just because of career risks

Coming out is a constant cost/benefit analysis and requires weighing different risks. A lack of support from coworkers and supervisors, and past experiences of discrimination, often prevent LGBTIQ+ workers from coming out. But our research also shows that respondents are more concerned about social exclusion than career risks. While about 19% of respondents who are not out at work said they worry their careers would be ruined if they were, 70% are concerned that coming out would make their colleagues uncomfortable around them.

The importance of a supportive social environment in a person's coming-out decision cannot be overstated. So what can organizations do to develop a workplace culture in which living authentically is an everyday reality for LGBTIQ+ workers?

Leadership Makes the Difference

Our research reveals that respondents whose leaders publicly support LGBTIQ+ issues are 50% more likely to be out to everyone at work. We recommend leaders who want to create an LGBTIQ+ inclusive culture:

- Develop a working partnership with leaders who have a different sexual orientation or gender identity than your own. This will help you learn, challenge your assumptions, and champion change.

- Make LGBTIQ+ inclusion visible in your organization. You can show support by displaying rainbow flags or other inclusive symbols, asking HR to create a diversity group where LGBTIQ+ people can connect and share their experiences, or developing a network of staff allies.

- Learn about all members of the LGBTIQ+ community. This means not just LGB people, but also people who are trans or gender diverse, who have an intersex variation, or who are pansexual.

- Check your assumptions to see if they hinder LGBTIQ+ inclusion. For instance: Everyone is straight; everyone prefers binary pronouns; coming out is a purely personal issue, not a workplace issue; this person must be LGBTIQ+ because of how they look, sound, dress, or behave; it's okay to "out" someone.

- Avoid noninclusive or presumptuous language, like "that's so gay" or asking women about their husbands and men about their wives, or assigning someone a gender pronoun. If you notice someone talking like this, take them aside and speak to them about it. When you do so, that person will be less likely to do it again and more likely to change their views on what is appropriate workplace behavior.

Organizations Must Also Step Up

Finally, we should point out that creating an LGBTIQ+ inclusive culture is not just about enlightened and supportive leaders. Organizational policies and strategies that recognize the specific needs—and sometimes just the existence—of LGBTIQ+ people are also key to establishing an inclusive environment.

We recommend that organizations:

- Include sexual orientation, gender identity, and intersex status in diversity and inclusion policies; have transition policies and supports in place for staff who are trans or gender diverse; and make sure parental leave policies recognize and include LGBTIQ+ people.

- Review workplace forms to ensure that they are inclusive and that they have an option for people who don't identify as either male or female.

- Designate some bathrooms as gender neutral, and introduce gender-neutral dress codes if your company has dress codes.

LGBTIQ+ people can be themselves and have a real choice about coming out at work when their employers and coworkers are supportive. Being aware of common assumptions and the challenges LGBTIQ+ people face is the first step toward building a work environment that is inclusive and safe for everyone.

Originally published on hbr.org in October 2018. Reprint H04LX6

Note

1. "LGBTIQ+" refers to lesbian, gay, bisexual, transgender/gender diverse, intersex, and queer. The "+" indicates that LGBTIQ doesn't include a range of other terms that people identify with or use to describe themselves.

About the Contributors

ROBERT D. AUSTIN is a professor of information systems at Ivey Business School and a coauthor of *The Adventures of an IT Leader* (Harvard Business Review Press, 2016).

KRISTIN BEHFAR is an associate professor at the Darden School of Business at the University of Virginia.

JEANNE BRETT is the DeWitt W. Buchanan, Jr., Distinguished Professor of Dispute Resolution and Organizations and the director of the Dispute Resolution Research Center at Northwestern University's Kellogg School of Management in Evanston, Illinois.

CATHY BROWN is a policy and research manager at Divinity Council Australia. Cathy has an undergraduate degree in Communications and a Master's in Social Inquiry from the University of Technology in Sydney with her thesis exploring issues for gay and lesbian seniors as they age.

NANCY M. CARTER is the senior vice president of research at Catalyst, a New York–based nonprofit that works with businesses to expand opportunities for women. She is also a visiting scholar at Insead.

FRANK DOBBIN is a professor of sociology at Harvard University.

ROBIN J. ELY is the Diane Doerge Wilson Professor of Business Administration at Harvard Business School and the faculty chair of the HBS Gender Initiative.

SYLVIA ANN HEWLETT is the founder and CEO of the Center for Talent Innovation and the founder of Hewlett Consulting Partners LLC.

HERMINIA IBARRA is a professor of organizational behavior and the Cora Chaired Professor of Leadership and Learning at Insead. She is the author of *Act Like a Leader, Think Like a Leader* (Harvard Business Review Press, 2015).

PAUL IRVING is chairman of the Milken Institute Center for the Future of Aging, the chairman of the board of Encore.org, and a distinguished scholar in residence at the University of Southern California, Davis School of Gerontology.

ALEXANDRA KALEV is an associate professor of sociology at Tel Aviv University.

MARY C. KERN is an associate professor at the Zicklin School of Business at Baruch College in New York.

JANE O'LEARY holds a PhD in Management and is a research director of Diversity Council Australia. Jane's research has appeared in the *Journal of Organizational Behavior* and *International Journal of Human Resource Management.*

CAROLYN BUCK LUCE is the executive in residence at the Center for Talent Innovation and senior managing director at Hewlett Consulting Partners. She is an adjunct professor at Columbia's Graduate School of International and Public Affairs and was previously the Global Pharmaceutical Sector Leader and Ernst & Young LLP.

GARY P. PISANO is the Harry E. Figgie Professor of Business Administration and the senior associate dean of faculty at Harvard Business School. He is the author of *Creative Construction: The DNA of Sustained Innovation* (Public Affairs, 2019).

CHRISTINE SILVA is a director of research at Catalyst.

DAVID A. THOMAS is the president of Morehouse College.

CATHERINE H. TINSLEY is the Raffini Family Professor of Management at Georgetown University's McDonough School of Business and the faculty director of the Georgetown University Women's Leadership Institute.

RAYMOND TRAU holds a PhD in Management and is a lecturer (equivalent to assistant professor) at RMIT University in Melbourne, Australia. Raymond's research has appeared in outlets such as *Journal of Applied Psychology, Human Resource Management,* and *British Journal of Management.*

CORNEL WEST is Professor of the Practice of Public Philosophy at Harvard University and professor, Emeritus, at Princeton University.

JOAN C. WILLIAMS is a Distinguished Professor of Law and the founding director of the Center for WorkLife Law at University of California Hastings College of the Law.

MAXINE WILLIAMS is Facebook's global director of diversity.

Index

Invaluable insights
always at your fingertips

With an All-Access subscription to
Harvard Business Review, you'll get
so much more than a magazine.

Exclusive online content and tools
you can put to use today

My Library, your personal workspace for sharing,
saving, and organizing HBR.org articles and tools

Unlimited access to more than 4,000 articles in the
Harvard Business Review archive

Subscribe today at hbr.org/subnow

The most important management ideas all in one place.

We hope you enjoyed this book from *Harvard Business Review*. Now you can get even more with HBR's 10 Must Reads Boxed Set. From books on leadership and strategy to managing yourself and others, this 6-book collection delivers articles on the most essential business topics to help you succeed.

HBR's 10 Must Reads Series

The definitive collection of ideas and best practices on our most sought-after topics from the best minds in business.

- Change Management
- Collaboration
- Communication
- Emotional Intelligence
- Innovation
- Leadership
- Making Smart Decisions

- Managing Across Cultures
- Managing People
- Managing Yourself
- Strategic Marketing
- Strategy
- Teams
- The Essentials

hbr.org/mustreads